A
MASTER'S
PERSPECTIVE

ADRIAN IKEJI

B.Eng. (Hons.), MSc

Understanding Brexit Neomercantilism,
Rent-Seeking, The gig economy, and the International
Trade of an emerging West African economy

First published in Great Britain as a softback original in 2019

Copyright © Adrian Ikeji

The moral right of this author has been asserted.

Typeset in Minion Pro

Design, typesetting and publishing by UK Book Publishing

www.ukbookpublishing.com

ISBN: 978-1-912183-77-7

I dedicate this book to my son Alexander who warmed my heart with the question "what is daddy doing?" on the 23rd of June 2016 - a moment before I voted in the United Kingdom Referendum on European Union membership. His question inspired the overarching perspective that led to my research papers contained in this book, for posterity.

"All knowledge of cultural reality, as may be seen, is always knowledge from particular points of view" – **Max Weber**

"To a person of analytical ability, perceptive enough to realise that mathematical equipment was a powerful sword in economics, the world of economics was his or her oyster in 1935. The terrain was strewn with beautiful theorems begging to be picked up and arranged in unified order" – **Paul Samuelson**

"This is one of those occasions in which the imagination is baffled by the facts" – **Adam Smith**

"So let's explore the fascinating interface between economics and politics together, with a heuristic approach, starting with a current First World conundrum with dynamic ramifications – Brexit. We may then traverse the ubiquitous nature of rent-seeking, and consider a peculiar modern trend in employment (for the benefit of millennials everywhere), before finishing off the expedition of discernment with a paper on a developing nation of interest. You're welcome" – **Adrian Ikeji**

Table of Contents

PAPER 3   **120**

PAPER 4   **140**

PAPER 1

Testing the impact of neo-mercantilism on UK trade globalisation before Brexit

By: Adrian Ikeji B.Eng. (Hons.), MSc.

Date: 05/12/2017

Abstract

As the United Kingdom (UK) leaves the European Union, this research tests the effects of neo-mercantilism in two ways.

First, from an econometric perspective to create a model for the trade openness and neo-mercantilism nexus, and secondly from the political angle presented by the Brexit conundrum, which represents a test of EU neo-mercantilism and UK trade globalisation in more practical terms.

Statistically significant relationships between trade openness and three indicators of neo-mercantilism were identified, namely: GDP per capita, interest rates and balance of trade. The relationship between GDP per capita and trade openness emerged as the most practically meaningful framework for assessing the future impact of Brexit on the UK economy. Furthermore, the relationship between balance of trade and trade openness may provide a contributory rationale for the emotional decision by a significant part of the electorate to vote for Brexit.

Suggestions from academic experts in International Trade and the EU Business Environment converged to present an unequivocal need for a government transitional agreement replicating the benefits of EU single market membership, as closely as possible. Their responses also capture the need for more visible and credible political leadership as soon as possible, to mitigate the economic uncertainty and to clarify the political ambiguity that is hampering the chances of galvanising the support in the polity required to secure a more competitive and beneficial path for the economic future.

The cumulative outcome of the mixed methodology employed in this research is a clearer picture of the motivations, means and mission for achieving a successful future in the UK political economy, post-Brexit.

Background to Brexit

(March 2017 Snapshot)

Mrs. Theresa May (MP), the Prime Minister of the United Kingdom (UK), sent a formal letter to the President of the European Union Council, on the 29th of March 2017 to trigger Article 50 (2) of the Lisbon Treaty, commencing the two-year process of negotiating an exit from the European Union (EU) – a political economic union and the largest trading bloc and largest single economy in the world – with purchasing power parity estimated at $20.8 trillion (CIA World Fact book 2016).

The letter follows on from the outcome of the democratic (Brexit) referendum held on the 23rd of June 2016 in which 51.9% of the UK electorate which translates to a 61% majority of Parliamentary Constituencies voted to leave the EU. Prior to the referendum, the UK Prime Minister, Chancellor of the exchequer, Governor of the Bank of England (BoE), several business leaders and economic experts predicted dire economic consequences (including an economic recession) for the UK economy and a quantified fall in the living standards for all UK households soon after the vote, because of the economic and political uncertainty that would ensue if we voted to leave the EU.

However, the advice and predictions were ignored by a majority of the electorate because of a plethora of reasons such as: a perception of uncontrolled immigration (from the EU); a growing perception of the loss of sovereignty; a perception of stagnating wages and increasing wealth inequality; the growing resentment against Multinational Enterprises and Banking Institutions since the 2008 financial crisis; the undemocratic nature and the lack of transparency surrounding the EU political integration plan; news of perennial economic and political crises in the

Eurozone; a perceived crisis of legitimacy and confidence in the leadership of the EU; increasing distrust of the political establishment in the UK etc.

There also appeared to be an optimistic and populist will to try the alternative espoused by leaders of the Vote Leave and Leave.EU Campaign teams - A post-Brexit vision that takes back control of the nation's borders, reduces financial contributions to the EU, returns legal sovereignty to parliament, enables bilateral free-trade deals to be agreed to realign the UK economy with emerging markets and the commonwealth, to stimulate economic growth.

To a large extent, the reasons for the referendum outcome closely mirror some of the problems with globalisation outlined by Bello (2004).

It has now been several months since the referendum result and although the UK has not yet negotiated the full terms of exit and a new relationship with the EU - and other current and potential future trading partners, most politicians and economists are surprised by the resilience and growth of the UK economy (apart from a 15% downward temporary correction in the currency exchange rate and a 2 - 4% rise in inflation predicted for 2017). The BoE growth forecast for 2017 has been revised back up to 2% last month, just as it was prior to the historically significant Brexit referendum.

Experts are also still surprised by the election of President Trump in the United States of America (USA), who dubbed his 2016 election campaign Brexit +++, as he sought to capitalize on the perceived anti-establishment (anti-globalisation) movement in the UK and USA, and did.

Could the phenomenon unfolding in the UK and USA mark a shift away from the neo-mercantilist experiments favoured by trading blocs and indicate the start of a new boost to trade globalisation which is characterised by genuine free trade?

Can the UK government actually deliver the balanced deal that reconciles the will of the electorate?

Could Frexit be next?

1. Introduction

It may now be an opportune time for social scientists to study the political dynamics, economic ramifications and academic importance of the aspects of globalisation studies brought into focus by the unprecedented democratic decision by the United Kingdom (UK) to vote to exit (Brexit) the political and economic union of 28 member states: the European Union (EU).

The EU is arguably the greatest example of globalisation, in all its forms, according to Bello (2004). Johnson (1974) surmised that when the UK joined the European Common Market (ECM) in 1973, it was an example of the neo-mercantilist approach to international trade, rather than the free-trade theory which is widely accepted by foremost economists, since the days of Adam Smith and David Ricardo, as being the most beneficial and productive path to economic growth.

The UK's exit may trigger an existential political crisis in the EU if other member states follow the UK example (but I expect they will not be able to afford to); the situation could redefine the strategic economic interests of a leading trading nation – one of the top 10 for imports and exports currently (according to the World Bank World Integrated Trade Solution Data for 2015), and may usher in a new era of free-trade and provide a new template for further economic globalisation for rich and powerful nation states.

This research aims to explore some of the macroeconomic and political drivers of trade globalisation and statistically test the causal link between them, in the context of the UK economy since it joined the ECM, with a view to predicting the nature of future UK trade globalisation (or trade deglobalisation) or the effects of UK neo-mercantilism outside the EU.

In essence, this research tests the effects of neo-mercantilist economic theory on a sovereign nation's trade openness – to explore the causal relationship between an important aspect of the globalisation phenomenon within a specific context. This is in order to learn more about an area of personal and national interest (Brexit) and to identify constructive suggestions for the uncertain path ahead, in light of the trade globalisation – neo-mercantilism nexus in the UK.

The ramifications of technological innovation, human capital development, environmental issues, migration trends, currency exchange rate fluctuations, Inflation, legal permutations, ideological globalism, neo-colonialism and neoliberal market capitalism are beyond the scope of this research.

Hill (2014 p5) states that," Globalization refers to the shift towards a more integrated and inter-dependent world economy". Facets of which include globalisation of markets, production, trade etc. However, economic deglobalisation was best described by Bello (2004 p113) as follows: "Deglobalization is not about withdrawing from the international economy. It is about reorienting economies from the emphasis on production for export to production for the local market...not leaving strategic economic decisions to the market but making them subject to democratic choice".

At this point in time, it is unclear which of the two paths the UK economy will take, if the will of the people on Brexit is implemented by the government.

Political rhetoric from the UK government since the Brexit referendum result in 2016 has been largely about leaving the EU single market and customs union potentially, whilst taking back control of borders and sovereignty. This alludes to a fascinating mixture of the phenomena defined above and may actually be achievable through genuine international free-trade outside the EU (and its neo-mercantilist tariffs and non-tariff barriers) combined with a new deal with the EU. Time will tell whether this ambition becomes an unprecedented achievement or remains illusory.

Johnson (1974 p14 -15) described the European Economic Community as the epitome of modernised mercantilism and posited that the main economic motivation behind the UK's membership of the ECM was essentially for protection against the "most dangerous competitor, American Industry.", in spite of the opportunity costs to UK consumers.

One could argue that in leaving the EU, after the two year period of exit negotiations ending in March 2019, the UK may be returning to the aspirations of the free-trade principles it pioneered. Or it may be repositioning its economy in a Porterian model of national competitive advantage to enhance the benefits of neo-mercantilism for itself and its citizens, and herald a future of economic prosperity in the long-run, post-Brexit.

It is widely accepted that globalisation of markets and production in the last decade, according to Hill (2014), have led to a surge in foreign direct investment (FDI), faster growth in world trade than world output (as some trade barriers continue to fall), deeper penetration of imports in developed economies and increasing competitive pressures within industries, but some EU member economies have fared better than others. For example, the German economy has record trade surplus levels while the UK has had correspondingly high trade deficits, which may or may not be related but is of concern as it impacts domestic manufacturing jobs, for example.

Therefore, a case study on the relevant aspects of the UK macro-economy could provide a unique insight on the empirical relationship between globalisation and some of its identified drivers. Especially as the UK economy has a widening deficit on trade in goods and services (estimated by the Office of National Statistics (ONS) at £4.2 billion in November 2016 alone) and the lowest ever Bank of England (BoE) official interest rate of 0.25%. Matters are further complicated by the political direction of the government of the day.

The research questions posed by this research are thus:

a) What has been the statistically significant relationship between UK trade globalisation and the following macroeconomic indicators, identified in the literature review, over the neo-mercantilist period of EU membership from 1973 to 2016? The indicators are: i) Inward FDI flow ii) Outward FDI flow iii) GDP per capita iv) Trade Balance v) BoE base rate of interest vi) Main Political Party in government

b) Why may neo-mercantilism be a contributory factor to Brexit?

c) What should the objectives of UK international trade policy be post-Brexit?

The first two questions are addressed from a quantitative research paradigm and the last question is addressed from a qualitative research paradigm for reasons described in the methodology section after the literature review identifies the research gaps.

2. Literature Review

This research explores the effects of some conceived indicators of a neo-mercantilist member state: the UK economy, in relation to its dynamic trade openness. The trade openness is approximated by the UK's trade globalisation over the past four decades, with a view to mapping trends over the period and estimating the nature and predictors of future change in openness or growth, if trade agreements are transformed post-Brexit.

This literature review provides the justification for the postulated indicators identified in an extensive body of relevant academic research and provides the basis for my quantitative analysis designed to address the first two research questions set out in the introduction. The third question is addressed in the qualitative part of the research, pursuant to the deductive work by me, and builds on the decision-making framework designed by Dhingra and Sampson (2016), to choose a sustainable post-Brexit path or predict a pattern for UK trade globalisation. Policy choices by the UK government since the Brexit referendum result have created a research gap in the aforementioned academic paper.

Trade globalisation is a measure of economic integration that represents the proportion of all production that crosses the boundaries of a country, as well as the number of jobs in that country dependent upon external trade or the proportion of the country's total volume of trade to its Gross Domestic Product (GDP), as described by Baccaro (2011).

It is operationalised as (Imports + Exports) / GDP. Trade globalisation, trade openness, trade openness percentage, openness index and trade to GDP ratio are commonly used names referring to the same concept.

Trade globalisation is underpinned by a system of regional rules and agreements, global rules and international institutions according to Bello (2004), such as the World Trade Organization (WTO), the United Nations Conference on Trade and Development (UNCTAD) and the World Customs Organization (WCO).

In the Blackwell Companion to globalization, Babones (2008 p147) states that trade globalization is by far the most commonly used indicator of a country's level of globalisation in empirical literature. He argues that trade is superior to investment for operationalising globalization because it captures many non-economic aspects of globalisation and is far less volatile than investment and therefore easier to measure.

Dinu et al (2015) refer to the Swiss Economic Institute (SEI) index of globalization which covers a wide range of issues indicative of globalisation and deglobalisation including economic, social, political and cultural globalization alongside the dynamics of import and export flows as an expression of international commerce, the dynamics of expats' money remittance and inflows and outflows brought by foreign direct and portfolio investments.

The SEI Index highlights the globalisation level of a national economy. Unfortunately, the data is only computed up to 2011 because it focuses on the impact of the 2008 financial crisis and Dinu et al posit that the slowdown in the globalisation process evidenced by the SEI Index could be considered to be a start of deglobalisation with short term effects experienced by developed states such as the UK.

Their predictions may be invalidated by the game-changing events of 2016 in the UK, which may arguably be linked to the 2008 financial crisis, because pre-crisis growth rates were only just returning to the economy.

Coupled with the new political shocks of the outcome of the Brexit referendum, trends are now more likely to have long-term effects on the political economy of the UK, which may provide a clearer indication of the nature of trade deglobalisation in the future. This research will go some way to addressing this research gap.

I believe trade openness is an apt dependent variable for all the reasons outlined above and because of the fact that proponents of the opposing sides of the Brexit debate have predicted a contraction of UK international trade and influence, post-Brexit, on the one hand and an expansion on the other. So I think it can be a useful indicator of economic fitness and the economic impact of Brexit.

Theoretically, the outward-facing or inward-looking orientation of the UK economy is based on a complex mix of economic issues including trade policy regimes, openness to investment, importation of goods and services and physical infrastructure. This is evidenced and tracked in the open market index prepared by the International Chamber of Commerce which represents businesses in Europe and around the world, and it interacts directly with the WTO.

The trade policy regime germane to this research is neo-mercantilism and is analysed critically next.

Characterisation of EU neo-mercantilism

The new form of mercantilism, in focus, is concerned not with the crude nation-state building or the provision of employment as such (although both elements have their place in the underlying philosophy) but with the economic growth and high living standards based on technical superiority in new industries, according to Johnson (1974).

The methods often abandon protection from imports in favour of fiscal subsidization of new import-competitive industries and high-technology potential export industries.

Harry Gordon Johnson went on to surmise that countries adopting the neo-mercantilist economic approach, look to the creation of supra-national protected market areas, rather than the protection of home markets synonymous with classical mercantilism. The evolution, expansion and further integration of the EU project over the last 44 years proves the accuracy of his prediction to some extent, and I seek to understand some of the underlying dynamics better, through my part-deductive case study covering new research ground.

During the era of neoliberal globalisation, i.e. since the 1970s, the majority of industrialized and emerging economies have reconfigured the combination of their economic policy instruments so as to foster external competitiveness, according to Hill (2014).

McFadzean (1972) argued at the British-American Chamber of Commerce in New York that the UK entry to the European Common Market would help to make the European community of nations more outward-looking and less inwardly absorbed in its own concerns, as a way of convincing countries outside Europe (including the USA) that european unity really is in the interest of the rest of the world, at a time when the consensus regarding the beneficial impact of trading blocs on international trade openness was unclear at best, despite the political rhetoric.

Hager (1987) argued that for Western Europe, continent-wide free-trade and a mixture of Japanese style internal competition and external protectionism would provide a neo-mercantilist answer to the dangers of deflation and loss of socio-economic autonomy posed by the mercantilist constellation of the world economy. He posits that this would provide a margin for macroeconomic policy and profitable investment to tackle unemployment and enhance industrial modernization.

A broader definition of neo-mercantilism is put forward by Guerrieri and Padoan (1986) which includes macroeconomic, monetary and trade components of mercantilist (economic and nationalistic) policies as a strategy based on a number of mutually supporting political and economic justifications. They reiterate the Keynesian idea in support of maintaining a positive current account balance, by suggesting that the inflow of liquidity generated by a surplus stimulates investment and therefore sustains employment because, given the marginal efficiency of capital and wages, this inflow leads to a decline in interest rates.

They do also suggest that globally however, these justifications may be considered as different and complementary ways of increasing both domestic welfare and stability and state power; arguably to ultimately create an autarkic super-state.

Their article describes the inevitable choice between neo-mercantilist restriction and co-operative expansion, faced by the major economies as the oligopolistic competition in the global economy intensifies between the leading economic powers today; a choice brought into focus again in the UK following the Brexit vote. It appears to me that the UK seeks to combine the benefits of both options.

According to Raza (2007), the overall objective of the EU neo-mercantilist trade policy is achieving, through trade negotiations, a final balance of offensive versus defensive interests that is considered to be generally advantageous by the main political actors in the EU. Offensive interests include sectors where European Companies are actively seeking improved market access and thus contribute towards increasing trade surpluses by exporting certain agricultural products, manufactured goods and professional services. Defensive interests include sectors where domestic economic interests call for protection against competition from third-countries e.g. Agriculture, Healthcare and other not-for-profit public services.

Raza (2007) surmises that EU trade policy has been aimed at increasing its net exports while applying selective import restrictions to protect sectors such as Agriculture which has a mean tariff of 30% to stimulate local production. Protection has been particularly high regarding agricultural inputs - commodities requiring further processing within the EU like Sugar, which has a mean duty of 350%; Milk and Milk products with a mean duty of 87%; grains with an average duty of 53% etc. The EU Common Agriculture Policy (CAP) is described as the most significant non-tariff barrier (NTB) to international trade in agricultural commodities with Europe by Krueger (1987) because it results in not only uneconomic domestic production of agricultural commodities but even in state subsidized exports.

Through this neo-mercantilist policy the EU trading bloc has profited immensely from the debt and import driven economic growth of the USA over the past three decades and the economic boom in China, according to Raza (2007) but, it may be adversely affected economically if the growth trends prove to be unsustainable.

With this backdrop, understanding the economic rationale behind the decision by the UK to negotiate a new deal with the EU and others becomes easier and urgent, if the opportunities presented by the 2016 referendum outcome are to be realised.

In order to measure the impact of the neo-mercantilist trade policies on the trade openness of an EU member state, on the verge of leaving the union, it would therefore be reasonable to consider the nature of the relationships between the aforementioned characteristic effects alluded to above i.e. Foreign Direct Investment (FDI), Economic Growth (GDP per capita), Balance of Trade, Interest Rates and Politics on Trade Openness, in the following subsections.

Foreign Direct Investment and Open Economies

Cooper (1986, p1155) defines open economy macroeconomics as "the sub branch of macro-economics that allows for International Trade in goods and services and for movement of capital across national boundaries in response to economic incentives."

He adapted the closed macroeconomic framework which presents national income as a function of national output and rate of interest, and proffered a framework in which national income is a function of total expenditure and the trade balance, for studying open economies. His work also highlighted the impact of flexible currency exchange rates in open economies, the relevance of which is beyond the scope of my investigation.

According to Kim and Lin (2009), by increasing the size of the market, trade openness allows the economies to better capture the potential benefits from increasing returns to scale and economies of specialisation.

However, opening up an economy to trade might actually reduce long-run growth if an economy specialises in sectors with dynamic competitive disadvantage in terms of potential productivity growth.

A study by Wang et al. (2004) on the impact of openness on growth in different country groups, by earnings, indicates that FDI is relatively more beneficial to high income countries like the UK, while international trade is more important for low income countries. The study confirms that the impact of openness on economic growth is influenced by a country's absorptive capacity therefore high and middle income countries are capable of benefiting from both international trade and FDI because of the high level of human capital.

The overall results of the empirical study suggest that trade openness is a multi-dimensional process characterised by the international flow of goods and services, the international movement of capital and transmission of ideas.

Liu and Li (2005) describe FDI as an important facet of globalization and detect a strong inter-determined endogenous relationship between FDI and economic growth from the mid-1980s to 1999 on a panel of data from 84 countries (including the UK) with no statistically significant relationship detected between 1970 and 1985. The study shows that there is a strong complementary connection between FDI and economic growth in both developed and developing countries.

Using a panel data-set of 35 economies over a 24 year period (1981 – 2004), Aspergis (2009) established the empirical finding that inward foreign direct investment does exhibit a significant long-run relationship with outward foreign direct investment in developed and developing countries. He also found that bi-directional causality is present in developed and open economies (including the UK). The results suggest that outward FDI is a key factor for enhancing growth prospects of an economy through plans for attracting FDI that will in turn move the economy onto higher levels of growth and openness.

Forte and Moura (2013) review the existing theoretical and empirical literature on FDI and economic growth and conclude that the effects of FDI on economic growth depend on the domestic conditions of the host country in terms of the degree of openness of the economy, human capital, economic and technological conditions. Furthermore, host country governments have a key role in creating the conditions that allow for the leveraging of the positive effects or for the reduction of the negative effects of FDI on the host country's economic growth.

Their conclusion is consistent with the Porterian theory of national competitive advantage described by Hill (2014 p181), which is generated endogenously by a system of four broad and mutually reinforcing attributes of a nation, namely: factor endowments; demand conditions; related and supporting industries; firm strategy, structure, and rivalry. All of which can be influenced by two additional variables, chance and government intervention, that shape the environment in which local firms compete.

Although the importance of FDI has been proven conclusively in relation to economic growth, it remains unclear what impact it has on trade openness. The statistical analysis in this study will investigate this link also.

Evidently, Brexit can be perceived as a chance for more host nation intervention through government policies designed to ensure the competitiveness of the UK economy going forward. Therefore, it would be reasonable to expect that regardless of the relationship between openness and FDI, future increases will continue to be desirable and actively sought by the UK.

International Trade and Growth

Frankel and Romer (1999) carried out a comprehensive empirical investigation of the impact of international trade on standards of living. They identified instrumental variables to estimate the effect and their results suggested that trade has a quantitatively large, robust, statistically significant and positive effect on income i.e. International trade raises income. Their findings also show that increasing a country's market size and area (which can be achieved by joining a free-trading bloc like the EU) by one percent, raises income by one-tenth of a percent or more.

Furthermore, the empirical evidence shows that a rise of one percentage point in the ratio of trade to GDP increases income per person by at least one-half of a percent. This study provides strong evidence in support of trade-promoting policies.

However, Gries and Redlin (2012) explore the causal relationship between trade openness and economic growth further by examining the short-run and long-run dynamics in a panel causality analysis for 158 countries, over a forty year period. Their results suggest that the long-run causality between trade openness and growth runs in both directions and their additional analyses for income-grouped subpanels shows that high-income countries exhibit a positive relationship between growth and Openness. They conclude that the growth-led openness and openness-led growth hypothesis can only be supported for industrialized countries.

Conversely, cross-country differences in growth rates in Income Terms of Trade were shown to have a strong correlation with differences in per capita income growth by Ekholm and Sodersten (2002). They argue that Income Terms of Trade is a useful concept for analysing the link between trade and growth.

GDP per capita is preferred for this research because of the extensive empirical evidence and relatability to a layperson.

Thirlwall and Gibson (1992) surmise that in open economies, export demand is the main component of autonomous demand in the virtuous cycle of export-led faster growth (as it is a determinant of investment, requires imports and the larger the domestic market the lesser the importance of external demand in enabling economies to reap economies of scale in production), so that the rate of growth of exports governs the long-run rate of output to which investment and consumption adjust.

This research provides further empirical evidence to support what the nature of the unidirectional causal relationship between GDP per capita and trade openness actually has been in the UK during the period of EU neo-mercantilism. And it will also test the link between the balance of trade and trade openness. From the literature, a directly proportional and an inverse relationship are expected, respectively.

Political indicator

Also in a cross-country context, Wacziarg (2001) evaluates various theories of dynamic gains from trade empirically, in an attempt to explain the observed positive impact of trade openness on economic growth. In his analysis it is posited that FDI - as a proxy for technological transmission, and the quality of macroeconomic policies, each account for about 20 percent of the way in which trade openness affects growth by raising the ratio of domestic investment to GDP.

However, his study also shows weak evidence that the size of government (measured by the ratio of public consumption to GDP) constitutes a channel through which trade policy could affect economic growth negatively.

The political dimension alluded to by the last point may warrant further investigation and justifies the inclusion of a categorical variable for that in my study and future studies, in my opinion. This would be to explore and reflect the link between the political ideology regarding the size of government in a polarised parliamentary democracy with only two main political parties with a realistic chance of forming a government in the UK, and trade openness, in order to evidence a relationship, if one exists.

The Conservative Party and The Labour Party are the two main political parties in the UK. The former has historically favoured smaller sized governments and less market intervention than the latter. Both parties have had the largest share of the vote in all general elections since 1930, according to Rallings and Thrasher (2007 p59).

Regardless of which party was perceived by the electorate to have won the last general election that took place on the 8th of June 2017, the new government (a Conservative minority government) now has a mandate to continue with the Brexit plan. Furthermore, they will inevitably have to make policy decisions to increase the national competitive advantage that may impact the chosen indicators and UK trade openness in the future, to possibly predictable degrees.

It is expected that the political aspects of this research are better explored qualitatively and are.

Relevance of Interest rates

Since the 2008 global financial crisis, BoE interest rates in the UK have been lowered to unprecedented levels as a mechanism to stave off inflation in the real economy (alongside quantitative easing and government spending cut-backs) and to boost economic growth.

A further link exists between the inflow of investment (FDI) and the level of BoE interest rates, as was alluded to earlier by Cooper (1986). However, interest rates have also been shown to be a strong indicator of future economic growth. In a research paper by Harvey (1991), an interest rate based model is shown to have substantially lower forecast errors than the traditional model used by the German Institute for Economic Research (DIW), at predicting economic growth and outperforms the consensus forecasts of five other major research institutes at predicting the economic growth of the German economy.

The term structure model used by Harvey correctly signalled all the economic turning points in the preceding twenty year period and is posited as a mechanism for mitigating the uncertainty that could hinder the business investment process and adversely impact future economic growth.

Furthermore, when considering an endogenous growth model, Gylfason (1993) argues that public policies to increase productivity and growth stimulate savings, and increase interest rates at the same time. The marginal productivity of capital and the rate of growth of output and other real variables in the long-run, are modelled in a way that allow them to be influenced by a number of variables including employment, trade policy etc. Gylfason concludes that the endogeneity of economic growth therefore opens a new channel through which governments may be able to influence interest rates and ultimately, economic growth.

This research posits a direct relationship between interest rates and trade openness. All the macroeconomic indicators above have been shown to impact economic growth and are affected by the overarching policy framework arguably described as EU neo-mercantilism. By extension, changes to the neo-mercantilist status quo will impact the trade openness because of the theoretical link identified.

The full analyses are presented in section 4.

Addressing the research gaps

It is reasonable to suggest that extensive research has been carried out on trade globalisation over the years and the same can be said about mercantilism - since trade liberalisation and free-trade became the consensus path to global prosperity for over a century.

However, more research is required to test neo-mercantilism because from the literature review it is evident that there is no consensus for its indicators and the nature of their relationship to trade openness. This research seeks to propose a predictive model that may be used to track macroeconomic changes in the UK post Brexit. It also aims to demonstrate an understanding of some of the effects of EU trade policy on the UK economy better through covering new research ground.

This research will show a trend for the econometric indicators in the long-term, if Brexit does not happen and may predict the likely trajectory of trade deglobalisation in the future under the status quo. It could also be used to justify a reversal by the government, if the post Brexit benefits fall short and become undesirable economically and politically in the future.

The statistical analysis may clarify the link between FDI and trade openness and provide further empirical evidence to support or quantify what the nature of the unidirectional causal relationship between GDP per capita and trade openness has actually been in the UK (supporting the growth led openness hypothesis) over the period of EU neo-mercantilism. All of which is unclear from the literature reviewed.

It may also put forward a link between interest rates and trade openness absent from the body of literature. And finally it may add to the decision-making framework presented by the experts at the Centre for Economic Performance prior to the 2016 Brexit referendum by positing a rational political choice on post-Brexit trade policy from the options available to the UK.

I have no doubt that globalisation, in all its forms, will continue and there is an increasing need for more sense-making research. The debate will rage on in the future regarding which approach to international trade delivers more benefits for consumers in the UK and globally, or whether a third way, a hybrid, is even possible in the short-run.

I expected to find statistically significant relationships between UK trade globalisation and the postulated neo-mercantilist macroeconomic indicators outlined above, before exploring the present political challenge that may shape trade policy in the UK for many decades to come.

3. Methodology and Methods

As a direct response to the nature of the novel and dynamic research problem of establishing a link between UK neo-mercantilism and trade globalisation from the period of EU membership through the present period of change and looking to the future, I have chosen to use a single holistic case study strategy from a part-deductive and part-inductive research approach, expatiated by Yin (2014). This is aimed to achieve greater intrinsic insight, reliability, internal validity and external validity; with the possibility of making statistical and analytical generalisations.

The research philosophy is akin to the post-positivist approach combined with the interpretivist approach and relativist ontology to posit a reality, based on pseudo-scientific statistical facts and understanding, enhanced by the experiential input from experts. The epistemology is subjectivist, which portrays a clear link between the flexibility of the researcher and the novelty of the subject-matter.

Basically, it is an exploration of economic reality through political arithmetic (statistics) passed through the prism in judgmental interviews to reveal political prose.

The justification for this approach is the likely unreliability of primary survey data for such a complex, relatively unexplored link between dynamic subject-matters, which have a high risk of not being strongly predictive or generalizable without more qualitative and quantitative studies.

There is also the latent ethical issue associated with interviewing a purposive sample about statistical analyses not carried out by them and introducing such a polarising and politically sensitive subject-matter at the moment, where ideological beliefs may dampen the propensity for objective qualitative insight. Therefore the quantitative framework is necessary, but is only capable of revealing tentative findings.

The research process started with the literature review of the theoretical background, which is followed by the collation and computation of numerical econometric data (and categorical political data) from the secondary data sets identified for the time-series analyses and described next. The full secondary dataset is attached as Appendix 1.

The data set for each test variable is described as follows:

Trade Openness Percentage: This is the sum of exports and imports of goods and services measured as a share of the gross domestic product for the year. The tabulated data found in Appendix 1, was computed from the World Bank and the OECD National Accounts data files. Appendix 1 also contains the descriptive statistics for the unprocessed model data set.

The graph below shows the pattern of fluctuations over the period of EU membership, with the best performance occurring in 2011 and a sharp decline since.

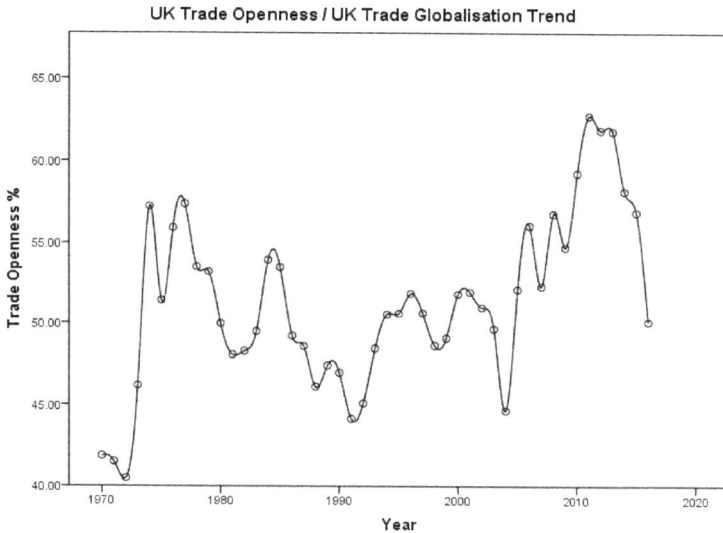

The higher the trade openness index, the larger the influence of trade on domestic activities and the stronger the country's economy as described by Baccaro (2011).

FDI-Inward: Net transactions in Equity Capital yearly totals were retrieved from the Office of National Statistics (ONS) Balance of Payments time-series data set (a positive figure means net liabilities increasing) and the World Bank data set, which shows net inflows of investment into the UK from the rest of the world in US$. Ownership of 10 percent or more of the ordinary shares of voting stock is the criterion for determining the existence of a direct investment relationship.

FDI-Outward: Net transactions in Equity Capital yearly totals were retrieved from the ONS UK Economic Accounts time-series data set (a negative figure means net assets abroad increasing) and the World Bank data shows net outflows of investment from the UK to the rest of the world in US$. The World Bank data set was the only complete set of FDI data I could find, from 1970 to 2016 and the values are in US$.

The graphs below show record levels of Inward FDI in 2016 and a slump in Outward FDI back to levels seen prior to EU membership.

Inward Foreign Direct Investment Flow in millions of US Dollars ($)

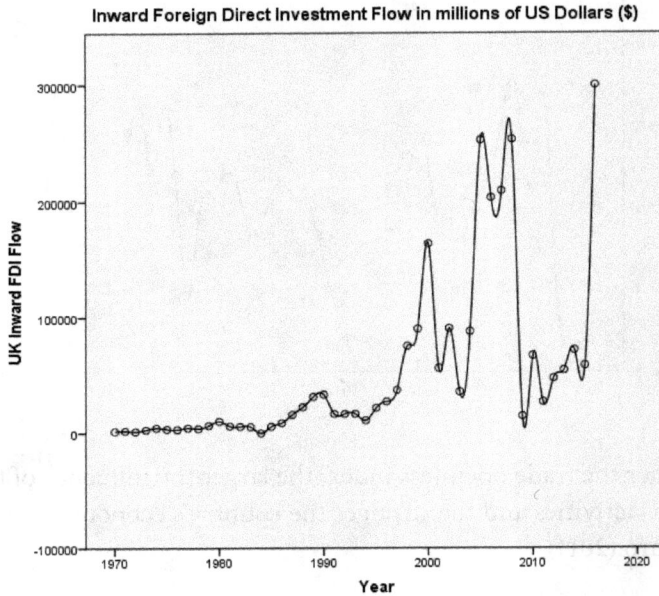

Outward Foreign Direct Investment Flow in millions of US Dollars ($)

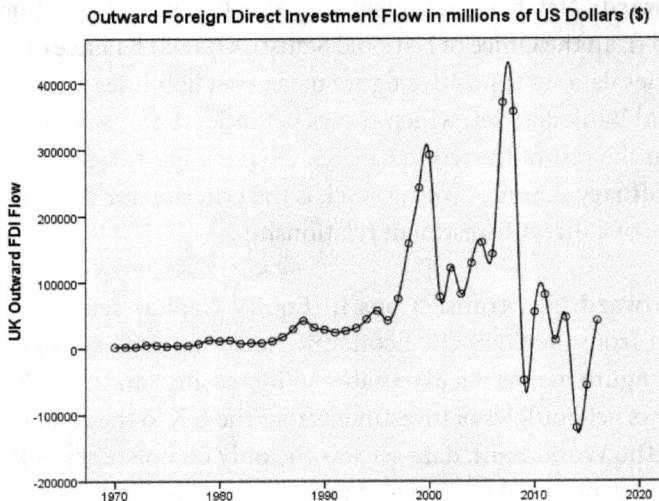

GDP per capita: The figures used are computed to the nearest pound from ONS annual GDP chained volume measures and population estimates. The graph below shows a constantly rising measure of total output with a dip after the 2008 global financial crisis and recovery from 2009 to the highest level in 2016.

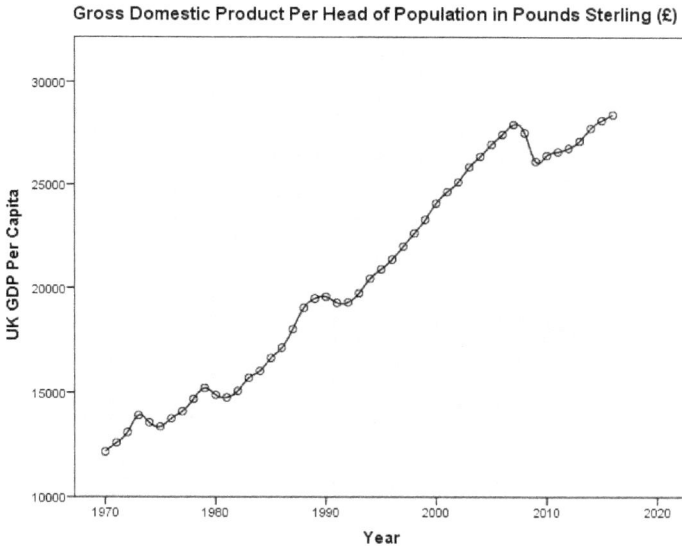

Gross Domestic Product Per Head of Population in Pounds Sterling (£)

Trade Balance: The annual totals were taken from the ONS Balance of Payments data set.

The graph below shows a persistent imbalance and larger trade deficits from 1997 onwards, with the largest deficit occurring in 2008 and largest trade surplus in 1981.

Differences in value of yearly Imports and Exports in millions of Pounds Sterling (£)

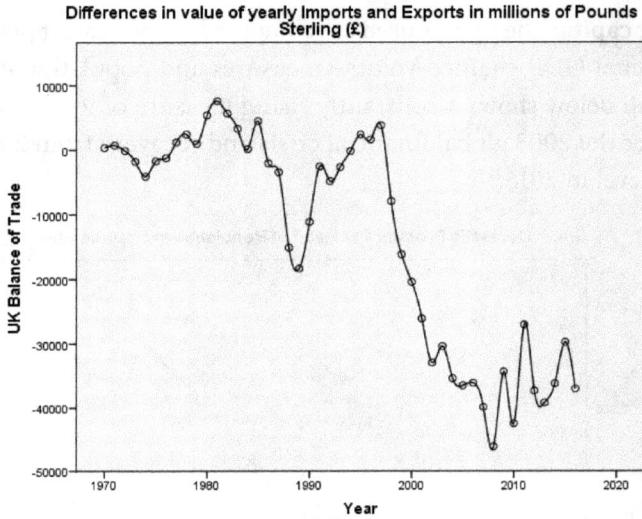

BoE base interest rate: The end of year BoE interest rate was selected for each year from the available BoE archived data sets. The graph below shows fluctuations with an historic slump to unprecedented low levels since 2008.

UK Bank of England Base Interest Rates

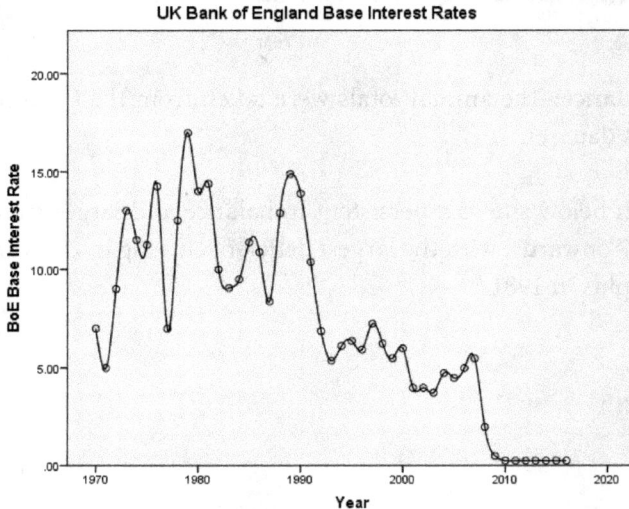

Governing Political Party data: The coding for the categorical data is 1= Conservative Party and 0 = Labour Party, as both parties have had the largest share of the vote in all general elections since 1930, according to Rallings and Thrasher (2007 p59). The chart below shows the political leanings in the country over the 47 year period up to the Brexit referendum.

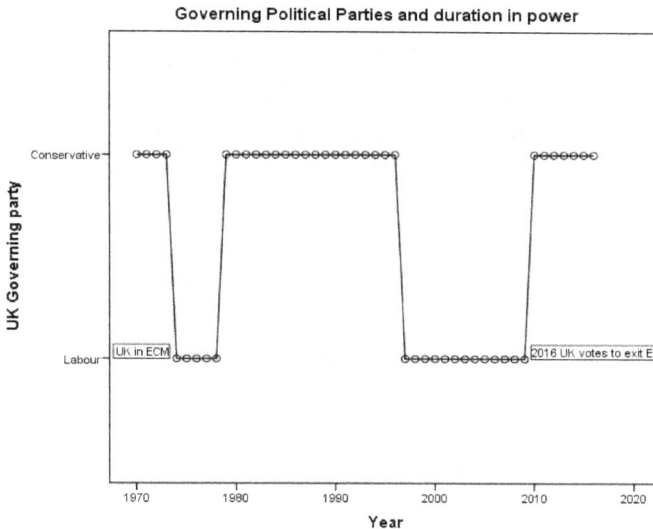

Governing Political Parties and duration in power

Statistical testing is done using the Ordinary Least Square Linear Regression method with the Statistical Package for Social Sciences (IBM SPSS computer software) to identify statistical significance, relative strength and direction of the relationships between UK trade globalisation and the explanatory variables of interest, identified in the literature review which may have practical significance.

All of the pre-testing assumptions for linear regressions are complied with and only a minor transformation was required for the dependent variable. However, the econometric data sets proved to be suitable regardless of the transformation, as the end results were unchanged. Evidence of the compliance with the pre-testing assumptions can be found in Appendix 2.

Following the evaluation of my results, qualitative primary data is collected with strict adherence and compliance with all stipulated ethical research protocols, from the purposive sample of academics with specialisations in International Trade and allied specialisms such as International Business and International Marketing. Semi-structured interviews were used after gaining informed consent, to explore some political aspects of the dynamic Brexit plans on future UK trade openness after extensive subject background research evidenced in section 4. The questions were modified through a dynamic iterative process while taking care to stick to the themes of interest.

This method of data collection was chosen because of the opportunity it presents to probe the answers given by the experts and to clarify or refine the questions dynamically in situ, where necessary, in order to funnel the learning outcomes in line with the research objectives.

An excerpt of the most elucidating interview transcript is included in the qualitative results after the note-worthy emergent themes are presented in a narrative analysis of the aggregated interview responses. This eliminates the need for further codifying the rich qualitative data on such a complex and dynamic area of study and mitigates the risk of introducing researcher bias which leads to more authoritative outcomes from the purposive sample.

The quantitative work can be best understood as the facilitator of the qualitative work, which I believe is a suitable approach for making economic theory more relevant and comprehensible in the real world.

This research creates a relationship between theory, different types of related data and the use of mixed research methods with a complementary purpose of increasing the understanding around a dynamic subject with an element of triangulation to validate the conclusions.

It would be inappropriate to seek to fully integrate data sets produced by different methods because they are underpinned by different sets of ideas about the nature of data, theories about the social world and so on, as described by Brannen (1992). This is the main reason for the stepwise research design adopted.

4. Analyses and Results

Quantitative Research Paradigm

This section focusses on the data set collected and analysed to answer the first two research questions. They are as follows:

a) What has been the statistically significant relationship between UK trade globalisation and the following macroeconomic drivers identified in the literature review, over the neo-mercantilist period of EU membership from 1973 to 2016? The indicators are: Inward FDI flow, Outward FDI flow, GDP per capita, trade balance, BoE base rate of interest and the main Political Party in government.

Hypothesis: The null hypothesis formulated to address the first question is H0 = There is no statistically significant relationship between UK trade openness and any of the selected independent variables. The alternative hypothesis, H1 = There are statistically significant relationships between UK trade openness and one or more of the independent variables.

b) Why may neo-mercantilism be a contributory factor to Brexit?

The answers to the questions will be made evident in the course of the analysis in the findings sub-section. The procedure used for the computational analysis is outlined below and followed by the inferential findings.

Test Procedure

After collating the data set without any missing values, scatterplots of the dependent variable (trade openness) against each continuous independent variable was generated. Lines of best fit were plotted to assess the linear relationships, the suitability of the collective data set for a Multiple Linear Regression (MLR) Analysis and the basis for the prediction model. Initial suitability of the data set was confirmed.

The stronger linear relationships were found to be between trade openness and balance of trade (with coefficient of determination, $R^2 = 21.4\%$), GDP Per Capita ($R^2 = 20.9\%$) and interest rate ($R^2 = 17.8\%$). The weaker relationships are with Inward FDI ($R^2 = 3.7\%$) and Outward FDI ($R^2 = 1\%$). The R^2 values reflect the goodness of fit and the lines of best fit for the squared errors associated with each data point are represented by the following equations:

1. $Y(\text{Trade Openness}) = 49.38 - 1.41\text{E-}4X(\text{Balance of Trade})$
2. $Y(\text{Trade Openness}) = 42.21 + 4.42\text{E-}4X(\text{GDP Per Capita})$
3. $Y(\text{Trade Openness}) = 54.67 - 0.47X(\text{BoE Interest Rate})$
4. $Y(\text{Trade Openness}) = 50.59 + 1.34\text{E-}5X(\text{Inward FDI})$
5. $Y(\text{Trade Openness}) = 51.18 + 2.06\text{E-}6X(\text{Outward FDI})$

The scatterplots were also grouped or split using the categorical variable (representing the political party) but the plots did not show any discernible pattern. Therefore showing no clear evidence that economic trends have been dependent on the governing political party over the sample period.

Thereafter, a multivariate normality test, homoscedasticity test, autocorrelation test and multicollinearity test were computed in turn to ensure compliance with the underlying assumptions, for the linear regression results to be reliable.

Testing for statistical homoscedasticity was performed using the Breusch-Pagan test, which performs an auxiliary regression of the squared residuals on the independent variables and the Koenker Test which is similar but is less sensitive to small sample sizes. The natural logarithm transformation of the trade openness figures was used because of the small sample size and the results showed homoscedasticity, which is an important requirement for the MLR Analysis because it indicates that the degree of random noise in the dependent variable remains the same regardless of the values of the independent variable.

The scatterplot of the regression standardized Predicted Value against Residual was also generated and the variance of the error terms remained constant which confirms homoscedasticity visually.

A visual autocorrelation test was performed using the scatterplot of all the unstandardized residuals (prediction errors) over time, to check the compliance with the assumption of independent errors in the data set. There is no clear pattern in the random plot which signifies the absence of auto-correlation. The plot is presented in Appendix 2.

Testing for statistical multicollinearity between the independent variables was performed using an iterative process in SPSS during the MLR analyses to identify independent variables with high Variance Inflation Factors (VIF > 5) or tolerance test values (1/VIF < 0.2). This was done to rule out multicollinearity (a strong relationship between the predictors) of variables, which was likely to obscure the significance of other variables. More so, it was performed in order to improve the effectiveness of the final MLR testing model by trying to resolve any such problems with the data set and to reveal significant relationships in this particular test, as the sample size cannot be increased because of the limitation of the period of EU membership under investigation.

Multicollinearity was detected in the GDP per capita and balance of trade data sets with no statistically significant predictor in the first MLR test, but with a significant F statistic. The multicollinearity problem, homoscedasticity results and multivariate normality statistical test results are also presented in Appendix 2.

The tactic used to attempt to resolve the multicollinearity problem was dropping the strongly correlated independent variable (GDP per capita) from the MLR test model which yielded statistically significant model statistics (F statistic and R^2 values) but balance of trade became the only statistically significant predictor variable of trade openness at the 95% Confidence level, i.e.at significance level α, alpha = 0.05 (the probability of rejecting the null hypothesis by Type 1 error). The related p-value was 0.037 or 3.7%, which is less than the significance level alpha, so the null hypothesis of there being no relationship in the model could be rejected and the alternative hypothesis could be supported with this evidence because the confidence interval does not contain the null hypothesis probability value for the independent variable.

A bivariate correlation table was computed to better understand the collinear relationships in the test data set and it showed moderate positive relationships between trade openness and GDP per capita and moderate negative relationships with BoE interest rate and balance of trade.

Furthermore, GDP per capita showed a strong negative correlation with BoE interest rate and balance of trade. Balance of trade showed a strong positive correlation with Inward FDI and BoE interest rate, which implied a possible masking effect between the variables caused by duplicated predictability. The correlation table is attached as Appendix 3.

Further iterations of swapping the strongly correlated independent variables yielded alternative MLR models with GDP per capita and BoE interest rates being singular predictor variables as well, as feared, with p-values of 2% and 1.3%, respectively. However, the relative strength of the linear predictor relationships could not be determined from the standardised regression coefficients – Beta, as there was only one significant predictor in each model and the model slopes were contradictory, rendering the MLR results interesting, but an MLR equation seemingly impossible due to multicollinearity (strong bivariate correlations).

Therefore, simple linear regressions had to be performed to identify the nature of the unique relationships between the statistically significant independent variables and trade openness.

Quantitative findings

The findings from the three bivariate linear regression tests that followed the unsatisfactory MLR analyses are presented below and they all show statistically significant evidence to reject the null hypothesis, H0 and support the alternative hypothesis, H1:

Linear Regression Model 1

Model Summary[b]

Model	R	R Square	Adjusted R Square	Std. Error of the Estimate
1	.463[a]	.214	.196	4.68269

a. Predictors: (Constant), UK Balance of Trade
b. Dependent Variable: UK Trade Openness %

ANOVA[a]

Model		Sum of Squares	df	Mean Square	F	Sig.
1	Regression	268.527	1	268.527	12.246	.001[b]
	Residual	986.740	45	21.928		
	Total	1255.267	46			

a. Dependent Variable: UK Trade Openness %
b. Predictors: (Constant), UK Balance of Trade

Coefficients[a]

Model		Unstandardized Coefficients		Standardized Coefficients	t	Sig.	95.0% Confidence Interval for B	
		B	Std. Error	Beta			Lower Bound	Upper Bound
1	(Constant)	49.375	.877		56.307	.000	47.609	51.141
	UK Balance of Trade	.000	.000	-.463	-3.499	.001	.000	.000

$R^2 = 21.4\%$, which means that of the variability in trade openness can be accounted for by the moderately correlated relationship with balance of trade; with other factors accounting for the rest of the variability.

The difference between R^2 and the adjusted R^2 value is trivial (less than 2%) because the sample size is big enough i.e. the difference is greater with smaller sample sizes and more independent variables.

The model F statistic is significant as the associated p-value above is much smaller than 0.05, therefore Linear Regression Model 1 is statistically significant, so I can conclude that the correlation coefficient and coefficient of determination between trade openness and balance of trade is not zero (i.e. not a chance occurrence) and the alternative hypothesis can be supported.

The unstandardized coefficient for balance of trade = -0.000141 (with 95% Confidence Interval = -0.000222 to -0.000060). Therefore, the regression equation for model 1 is: **Y(Trade Openness) = 49.38 – 0.000141X(Balance of Trade)**

Model Prediction: One unit increase in trade surplus = 0.000141 decline in trade openness which means that if the balance of trade was zero then the UK trade openness would be equal to the Constant = 49.38 %.

The histogram and Probability to Probability (P-P) plot below show that the residuals of the regression are approximately normally distributed. This confirms the suitability of the regression model.

This finding makes sense, in light of the conclusion in Thirlwall and Gibson (1992) that the rate of growth of exports governs the long-run rate of output to which investment and consumption adjust. The definition of neo-mercantilism espoused by Guerrieri and Padoan (1986) also reflected the importance of maintaining a positive current account balance, by suggesting that the inflow of liquidity generated by a surplus stimulates investment and therefore sustains employment because, given the marginal efficiency of capital and wages, this inflow leads to a decline in interest rates.

So in essence, as UK exports increase and the trade deficits decrease then trade openness will also decrease, but with beneficial effects for domestic jobs creation and wage increases potentially.

This rationale may also provide some evidence to support the rational decision by sections of the UK electorate to vote for the change Brexit could bring, in the hope of gaining a positive economic dividend of globalisation. I suggest this also answers the second research question.

The histogram and Probability to Probability (P-P) plot below show that the residuals of the regression are approximately normally distributed. This confirms the suitability of the regression model.

Histogram

Dependent Variable: UK Trade Openness %

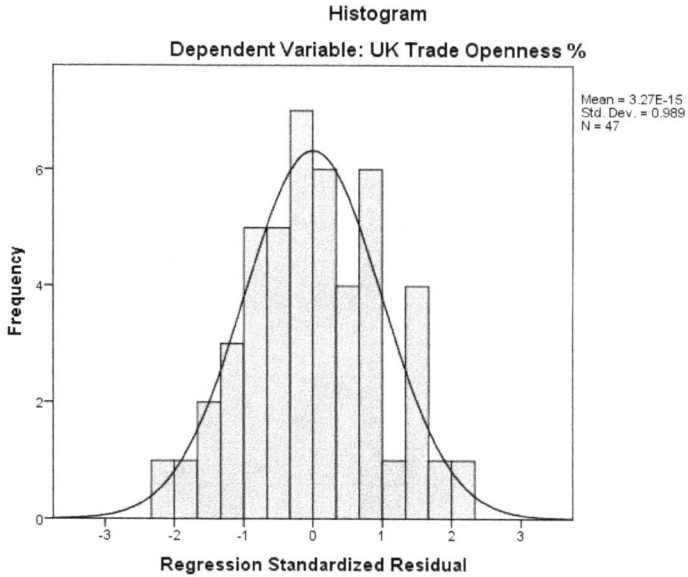

Mean = 3.27E-15
Std. Dev. = 0.989
N = 47

Normal P-P Plot of Regression Standardized Residual

Dependent Variable: UK Trade Openness %

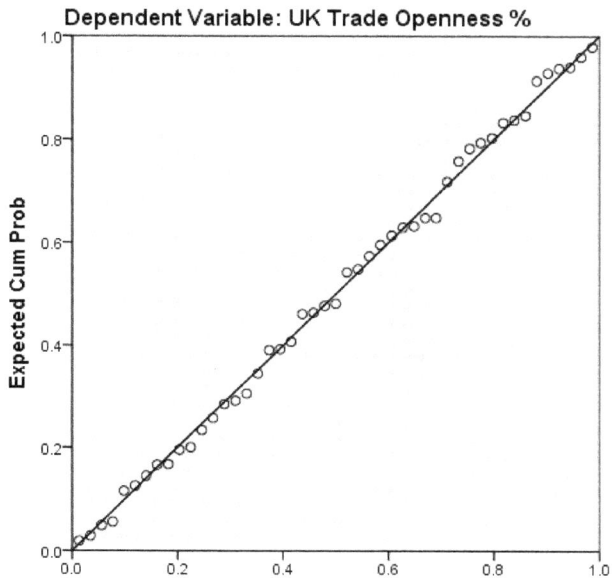

Linear Regression Model 2

Model Summary[b]

Model	R	R Square	Adjusted R Square	Std. Error of the Estimate
1	.458a	.209	.192	4.69599

a. Predictors: (Constant), UK GDP Per Capita

b. Dependent Variable: UK Trade Openness %

ANOVA[a]

Model		Sum of Squares	df	Mean Square	F	Sig.
1	Regression	262.912	1	262.912	11.922	.001b
	Residual	992.356	45	22.052		
	Total	1255.267	46			

a. Dependent Variable: UK Trade Openness %

b. Predictors: (Constant), UK GDP Per Capita

Coefficients[a]

Model B		Unstandardized Coefficients		Standardized Coefficients	t	Sig.	95.0% Confidence Interval for B	
		Std. Error	Beta			Lower Bound	Upper Bound	
1	(Constant)	42.212	2.719		15.522	.000	36.735	47.690
	UK GDP Per Capita	.000	.000	.458	3.453	.001	.000	.001

a. Dependent Variable: UK Trade Openness %

$R^2 = 20.9\%$, which means that of the variability in trade openness can be accounted for by the moderate relationship with GDP per capita.

The difference between R^2 and the adjusted value is trivial (less than 2%) because the sample size is big enough i.e. the difference is greater with smaller sample sizes. The F statistic is significant so the null hypothesis can be rejected as there is evidence to support the alternative hypothesis of a statistically significant relationship between the dependent and independent variable.

The unstandardized coefficient for GDP per capita = 0.000442 (with 95% Confidence Interval = 0.000184 to 0.000701). Therefore, the regression equation for model 2 is:

Y (Trade Openness) = 42.21 + 0.000442X (GDP per capita)

Model Prediction: One unit increase in GDP per capita = 0.000442 increase in trade openness, which means that if the GDP per capita was zero then trade openness would be equal to the constant = 42.21% (which has no practical meaning or significance). However, this relationship was somewhat expected partly because of the findings by Gries and Redlin (2012) which suggested the long-run causality between trade openness and growth runs in both directions and partly because of the reality of consumption driven growth in the UK economy over the past few decades.

The histogram and Probability to Probability (P-P) plot below show that the residuals of the regression are approximately normally distributed. This confirms the suitability of the regression model.

Histogram

Dependent Variable: UK Trade Openness %

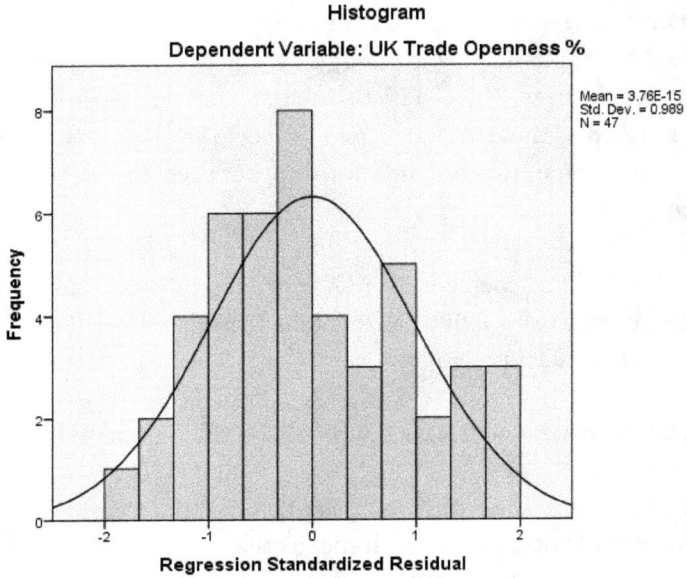

Mean = 3.76E-15
Std. Dev. = 0.989
N = 47

Frequency / Regression Standardized Residual

Normal P-P Plot of Regression Standardized Residual

Dependent Variable: UK Trade Openness %

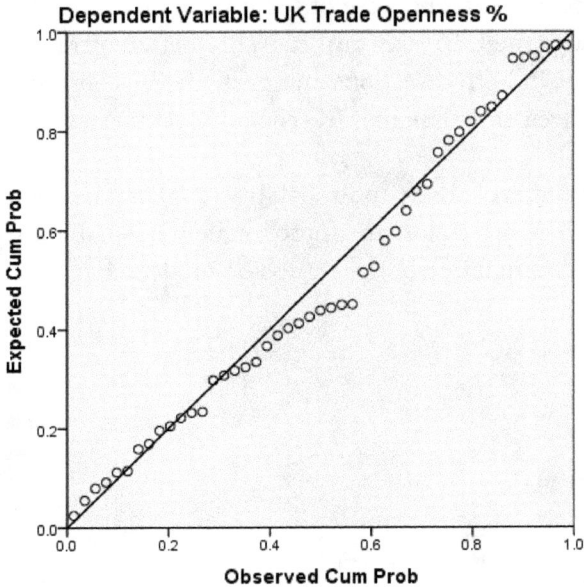

Expected Cum Prob / Observed Cum Prob

Linear Regression Model 3

Model Summary[b]

Model	R	R Square	Adjusted R Square	Std. Error of the Estimate
1	.422[a]	.178	.160	4.78891

a. Predictors: (Constant), BoE Base Interest Rate

b. Dependent Variable: UK Trade Openness %

ANOVA[a]

Model		Sum of Squares	df	Mean Square	F	Sig.
1	Regression	223.251	1	223.251	9.735	.003[b]
	Residual	1032.016	45	22.934		
	Total	1255.267	46			

a. Dependent Variable: UK Trade Openness %

b. Predictors: (Constant), BoE Base Interest Rate

Coefficients[a]

Model B	Unstandardized Coefficients		Standardized Coefficients	t	Sig. Lower Bound	95.0% Confidence Interval for B	
	Std. Error	Beta				Upper Bound	
1 (Constant)	54.671	1.287		42.484	.000	52.080	57.263
BoE Base Interest Rate	-.468	.150	-.422	-3.120	.003	-.770	-.166

a. Dependent Variable: UK Trade Openness %

R^2 = 17.8%, which means that of the variability in trade openness can be accounted for by the moderate relationship with BoE interest rate.

The difference between R^2 and the adjusted value is trivial (less than 2%) because the sample size is big enough i.e. the difference is greater with smaller sample sizes. The F statistic is significant so the null hypothesis can be rejected as there is evidence to support the alternative hypothesis of a statistically significant relationship between the dependent and independent variables.

The unstandardized coefficient for Base interest rate = -0.468 (with 95% Confidence Interval = -0.77 to -0.17). Therefore, the regression equation for model 3 is:

Y (Trade Openness) = 54.47 – 0.468X (BoE Interest rate)

Model Prediction: One unit increase in Base interest rate = 0.468 decline in trade openness, which means that if the BoE base interest rate was zero then UK trade openness would be equal to the Constant = 54.67 %

This appears to be the most economically significant finding because it provides evidence to suggest that interest rates may be lowered further in the short-run to stave off undesirable consequences of Brexit. This finding is also consistent with the assertion by Harvey (1991) that interest rates may be useful as a mechanism for mitigating the uncertainty that could hinder the business investment process and adversely impact future economic growth. It is also consistent with the neo-mercantilism definition by Guerrieri and Padoan (1986) referred to in the analysis of Linear Regression Model 1 above.

The histogram and Probability to Probability (P-P) plot below show that the residuals of the regression are approximately normally distributed. This confirms the suitability of the regression model.

Histogram

Dependent Variable: UK Trade Openness %

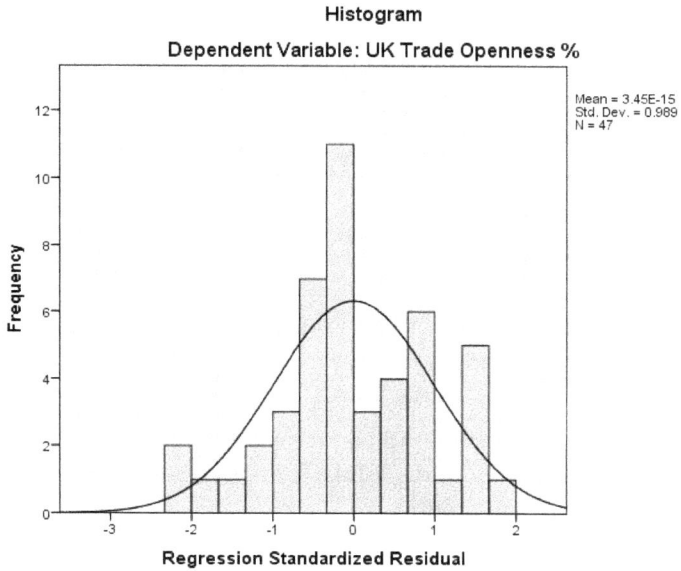

Mean = 3.45E-15
Std. Dev. = 0.989
N = 47

Normal P-P Plot of Regression Standardized Residual

Dependent Variable: UK Trade Openness %

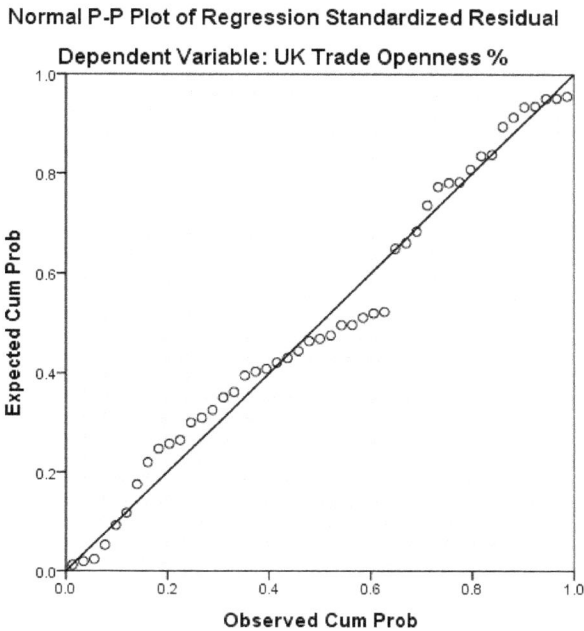

The other independent variables (Inward FDI, Outward FDI and Governing Political Party) did not show any statistically significant relationship with trade openness.

Inferential statistical model analysis

The corresponding model conclusions from the UK economy under the EU neo-mercantilist period are thus:

A) One thousand units increase in trade surplus which equates to one billion pounds = 1.41 units decline in trade openness percentage point which means that if the balance of trade was zero then the UK trade openness would be equal to 49.38 %. (0.7% less than 2016 figures).

B) One thousand units increase in GDP per capita which equates to one thousand pounds = 0.442 unit increase in trade openness; the GDP per capita data shows that such an increase has taken place recently, approximately every 2 years, and it would be interesting to see if this trend accelerates or slows down post-Brexit. This finding quantifies the growth-led openness hypothesis described by Gries and Redlin (2012).

C) One unit increase in the base interest rate = 0.468 decline in trade openness, which means that if the BoE base interest rate was zero then UK trade openness would be equal to the Constant = 54.67 % (4.5 percentage points above the current level of trade openness). This may suggest that a further cut to the interest rate is more likely than an increase in the short-run, after Brexit, and Harvey (1991) provides compelling evidence to rationalise this position.

The next section focuses on exploring the present political challenge that may shape trade policy in the UK for many decades to come, after the UK exits the EU. In essence, this method is used to shed light on how the challenges maybe overcome and the likely trajectory of UK neo-mercantilism outside the EU.

Qualitative Research Paradigm

The purpose of the interviews is to complement and build on the findings from my quantitative research into the macroeconomic effects of EU neo-mercantilism on the UK economy pre-Brexit. It is designed to answer the third research question, which seeks to identify a specific, relevant, measurable and time-bound objective of UK international trade policy post-Brexit.

The interviews are also intended to build on the framework of international trade options for the UK after Brexit, summarised in the "Life after Brexit" research paper from the London School of Economics - Centre for Economic Performance (CEP), by Dhingra and Sampson (2016). The options set out in the CEP paper include: joining the European Economic Area (the Norwegian model), forming bilateral treaties (the Swiss model), re-joining the European Free Trade Association (EFTA) and falling back on WTO rules.

However, all the options have been deemed unsuitable by the government and are incompatible with negotiation objectives set out by the UK government to date, in the Prime Minister's Lancaster House Speech on the 17th of January 2017 and the Article 50 Letter to the President of the European Council on the 29th of March 2017.

In the Lancaster House Speech by May (2017), it is claimed that since joining the EU, trade as a percentage of GDP has broadly stagnated (the data set used for this research shows trade openness in 1974 = 57.23% and 2015 = 56.85%), and the UK now wants to trade and do more business all around the globe and so Britain must not be part of the Common Commercial Policy or be bound by the Common External Tariff – two aspects of the EU Customs Union, which currently prevents the UK from negotiating and agreeing its own international trade agreements. Furthermore, the Article 50 letter by May (2017) sets out the ambition of achieving a free-trade agreement bigger than any previously agreed and includes financial services and networked industries to capitalise on the unique opportunities of regulatory alignment, the historical relationship of trust in one another's institutions and the spirit of co-operation between the UK and EU.

The main trade - related sticking points are the current lack of a comprehensive agreement on trade in services with third-countries outside the EU single market (which is particularly sensitive because of the proportion of the UK GDP made up by the services sector) and the foundation principle of Free Movement of people within the EU single market; positions which are problematic for the UK government for conflicting political and economic reasons considering the outcome of the Brexit referendum and the subsequent General Election result.

Politically, the government has to be perceived to be delivering the will of the majority of the electorate to forge a new relationship with the EU which addresses the concerns of a sense of diminishing sovereignty (and future fears), uncontrollable EU migration and rising income inequality. At the same time, giving up the economic benefits of EU single market membership is seen by most experts on record, potentially as an act of economic self-harm and the prospect of a new settlement which allows the UK to maintain significant benefits of the status quo and add significant increases to trade with third-countries, quite far-fetched.

Nevertheless, a more favourable and bespoke model is sought by the UK and the interviews shed light on the challenges, and solutions that could enhance to government's position and likelihood of success with Brexit.

Experts were selected with specialisations in International Trade, EU Business Environment, International Marketing and International Business. Three of the four requisite interviews took place (four further participation invitations were turned down by unavailable academic experts or ruled out by a new University policy prohibiting some Birkbeck experts from taking part). Consent for recording and publication was granted in two cases.

The main themes identified across the interviews are summarised below followed by an excerpt of the authoritative interview with the International Trade Specialist is included herein with the expert's permission, to give a comprehensive insight which is central to my research objective. An alternative (more pro-business) perspective is presented in Appendix 4 alongside the full transcript of the interview with the Trade Specialist.

Qualitative findings

Five semi-structured questions themes were posed to all the interviewees covering the following dilemmas facing the UK government. There was broad convergence of opinion in most areas with immaterial or subtle differences attributable to the interviewee's area of specialisation. The emergent thematic responses to the semi-structured questions are presented below:

1. **Line of questioning:** How effectively is the political consensus on Brexit being communicated?

Response Theme: All respondents agreed that there is a need for more coherent communication on what, how and why the government aims to achieve its Brexit objectives and there is a dearth of effective political leadership, regarding ruling the No-deal option in or out.

2. **Line of questioning:** What would be the likely effect of the UK not securing its trade deal objective with the EU?

   Response Theme: All respondents are confident that in the absence of a negotiated settlement, the UK would revert to WTO rules with a consequent slowdown in economic performance because of the predictable and asymmetrical shock to the services sector coupled with a reduction in living standards. All interviewees consider the possibility of Brexit not actually occurring as a complicated but conceivable prospect.

3. **Line of questioning:** Which Trade deal compromise is in the UK's best interest?

   Response Theme: The comprehensive free-trade deal proposed by the government was preferred by the interviewees over unilateral trade liberalisation but it is considered to be less beneficial than membership of the EU single market. Therefore by implication, any outcome that does not include membership of the single market will be seen as a backward step, and there was not much optimism regarding beneficial trade deals with emerging economies or third-countries.

4. **Line of questioning:** What is the most desirable Brexit strategy for UK businesses?

Response Theme: All the experts were in favour of a long transitional agreement and opposed to the idea of a clean break from the EU, principally because of the significant new costs to businesses that will ensue and the prevailing interconnectedness that has formed naturally in the single market over the years. Again, this option is considered to be the least bad option.

5. **Line of questioning:** Which relationship from the neo-mercantilist quantitative paradigm may be a meaningful lens for judging the impact of government policy on the economy after Brexit?

   Response Theme: All the respondents rationalised the link between GDP per capita and trade openness and tentatively suggest that the economic impact of Brexit is expected to affect this nexus rather than the two others identified in the quantitative analysis.

Trade Specialist Interview Excerpt

Precis of core questions by researcher (AI) and answers by expert 1 (TS) in grid below:

AI – What is your understanding of what happens if no New-Deal is agreed with the EU or if we just walk away from negotiations? Should it mean continued Single Market Membership with Customs Union concessions, immigration concessions and payments? Or WTO rules (as indicated in the Article 50 letter), with no defined government yearly payment to the EU but new costs for market access to businesses?

TS – What would happen if we don't have any deal before or by the end of March 2019, we leave without any kind of deal - from a trade perspective that would mean that we would then trade with the EU broadly speaking under similar terms as those with which we currently trade with countries like the USA or China which is to say under WTO terms.

That would mean there would be new tariffs on trade with the EU and it would also mean an increase in non-tariff barriers between the UK and the EU so if things like the passporting rights that allow financial services firms to operate throughout the EU, those would disappear so it would be harder for those firms to export their services.

So what I would expect to see would be a contraction in trade with the EU, which would reduce and have a negative effect on the UK economy relative to whatever would have happened in the alternative scenario and therefore it would leave the UK worse off than it would otherwise have been.

AI – Would you say it was at all possible that in the event that negotiations fail we could continue trading relations with the EU under the status quo?

TS - No I would say that if we don't get a deal and we don't withdraw our Article 50 notification, and there's a legal question regarding whether we even can withdraw it, then my understanding is that the default would be at the end of March 2019 for the UK to leave the EU and from that date we lose all the privileges and trading rights from being a member of the European Union.

AI – Excuse me Dr. Sampson, but would that also mean that all the Preferential Trade Agreements that were negotiated by the EU on behalf of the UK while it was a member of the single market, would have to be re-negotiated by the UK?

TS – Yes. Now how exactly that process would work is unclear because there isn't any precedent for this happening. My hope and to some extent expectation is that as long as there is goodwill on both sides, it would be relatively straight forward for the UK to get a deal with those countries that kind of essentially maintains the status quo of those relationships but that would be contingent on the other trading partner, so for example South Korea is a good example of a country that the EU has a free-trading agreement with; it would require South Korea's agreement to allow the UK to continue trading with it on those preferential terms and that will require some diplomatic work to get and may require some concessions from the UK.

AI – Is an early transitional agreement with the EU better for businesses than the certainty of an early no-deal? Why?

TS – That's a good question. The way I think about this is: if you think about what businesses are worried about here, there are two aspects to it.

First, businesses don't like uncertainty because it makes it hard for them to plan and that might mean that they delay investments and that reduces output.

The other thing is that we are not just facing uncertainty here, but we're facing actual new costs so even if they were certain that we were going to leave the EU with no deal that would still be a problem for business because that would mean that they would be facing new trade costs which would make it harder for them to trade with the rest of the EU and is bad for business. So those are two negative effects on businesses.

The certainty of an early no-deal solves the uncertainty problem but it doesn't solve the new costs problem. Whereas a transitional agreement, at least temporarily solves the problem of facing higher trade costs, if you assume that the transitional agreement is something like the status quo but it also means that you don't fully resolve the uncertainty because you're effectively just saying you push the uncertainty down the road.

It kind of depends which of those components of the problems businesses are facing or which is more important to the business and at least in the short-run I am not sure what the answer to that would be.

In the long-run I would probably say that the problem of higher trade barriers would be more problematic but in the short-run it is more difficult to predict.

AI – Lastly, of the three statistically significant findings from my quantitative research presented in the information sheet, which may be the most crucial indicator or relationship worth monitoring post-Brexit?

TS – I think the link between trade openness and income per capita is important and I see the relationship you have identified in your research.

The finding that countries that are more open for trade tend to have higher income per capita is backed by a large body of both theoretical and empirical evidence to support the fact that as countries become more open it has positive effects on income per capita and I think that is a useful frame for thinking about what the effects of Brexit are likely to be, in the sense that if the UK does close itself off and trades less with the rest of the world that will have negative income effects so I think that's a useful result for thinking about the likely economic effects of Brexit.

AI – But if the government were to take decisions within the economy that lead to a rise in GDP per capita that also has a positive effect on trade openness as demand for imports increases, so there is bi-directional causation, isn't there?

TS - I agree there is a two way relationship. The reason I stress the relationship from openness to GDP per capita is that I would see openness not as a goal in itself from an economics perspective, but as a means to an end.

What we care about in the end is welfare and living standards. Income per capita doesn't perfectly capture that but it is a useful proxy for thinking about it. Whereas, trade openness per se, I wouldn't care about trade openness unless it is affecting living standards so that's why I stress that side of the relationship.

5. Conclusions

From the qualitative research results, it is apparent that what the UK government needs to do to improve its chances of economic and political success through this current period of momentous change is to adopt a clearer communication strategy for its aims and objectives regarding Brexit. This is very important in the crucial months of negotiation ahead and beyond, and it needs to demonstrate a willingness to reach a compromise on minor issues in the interest of the common good for the UK and EU economies, so as not to jeopardise major ones (e.g. Trade).

Unfortunately, it still remains unclear at this point in time how the UK can be extricated from the EU Common Commercial Policy and the Common External Tariff mechanism without necessitating a politically sensitive customs border with the EU at the frontier with the Republic of Ireland, in order for the UK to negotiate and agree its own international trade agreements with third countries, which is a clear Brexit aspiration. Until this issue is resolved, the risk of no new deal with the EU or a reversal of the exit process will remain outcomes that are equally as likely.

However, a new trade deal with the EU which is characterised as a comprehensive free-trade deal or any other politically acceptable euphemism for single market membership, and a new friction-less customs arrangement, which allows for the bilateral trade deals with third-countries; complemented by a greater sense of democratic control at the national level, may yet prove to be an achievable compromise in the long-run; provided a mutually beneficial, lengthy and phased transitional-implementation agreement can be negotiated by the UK government by the end of March 2019.

This should be the primary objective for post-Brexit trade policy, which will deliver the best outcome for the UK and ultimately reveal how EU neo-mercantilism has led to UK neo-mercantilism, which could mean an even bigger global market for UK businesses, cheaper food, clothing and services for UK consumers and a stronger economic and political partner for the EU.

The UK could also benefit from more authentic leadership at the start of any formal implementation period to strengthen the political consensus in the country and provide the much needed political stability and certainty. This may be necessary in order to gain a clearer mandate from the electorate at the next general election to gain more continuity to build on the political and economic objectives in relation to international trade and economic growth while learning from the known lessons of the recent EU neo-mercantilist past.

The EU neo-mercantilist period researched has been shown to be characterised by increasing trends in trade deficits in the UK (and the contingent negative impacts on real wages and widening income inequality levels), as opposed to trade surpluses in the EU overall, which was an EU objective highlighted by Raza (2007).

This macroeconomic finding is in contradiction to the neo-mercantilist aims set out in the definition by Guerrieri and Padoan (1986), which may be a contributory rationale for Brexit and an answer to the second research question.The finding is consistent with the findings by Thirlwall and Gibson (1992), in that the rate of growth of exports governs the long-run rate of output to which investment and consumption adjusts. Although, some of the undesirable perceptions of trade deficits are mitigated by the Inward FDI trend, but the undesirable effects are real for the poorest groups in the UK labour market.

The period also showed rising trends in GDP per capita and falling trends in BoE base interest rates vis-a-vis a rise in the trade openness of the UK economy over the last 44 years.

This research identified three statistically significant predictive models for trade openness represented by the following regression equations analysed in section 4:

a. Y (Trade Openness) = 49.38 – 0.000141X (Balance of Trade) + Error; R^2 = 21.4%

b. Y (Trade Openness) = 42.21 + 0.000442X (GDP per capita) + Error; R^2 = 20.9%

c. Y (Trade Openness) = 54.47 – 0.468X (BoE Interest rate) + Error; R^2 = 17.8%

The percentage of variance in trade openness explained by the linear relationships is depicted by the R^2 values listed above. Trade openness has a moderate positive correlation with GDP per capita and moderate negative correlations with balance of trade and BoE interest rate. Trade deficits have a strong negative correlation with GDP per capita and Inward FDI, and a strong positive correlation with BoE interest rates. GDP per capita also has a strong negative correlation with BoE interest rates, so the R^2 values account for related variations (not cumulative), but causality remains unclear.

The most indicative of the relationships worth monitoring post-Brexit being the empirical link confirmed between GDP per capita and trade openness and favoured by the experts interviewed, as a useful framework for assessing the impact of Brexit on the welfare of UK consumers after the UK leaves the EU. While the other two relationships could form the basis for a comparative study examining changes in the trade openness - neo-mercantilism nexus, post-Brexit.

Other contributory factors that may be expected to impact the complex process of UK trade openness into the future include: new geopolitical alliances, further currency exchange rate fluctuations, global security challenges, labour migration flows, changes to capital flows, endogenous ease of doing business, technological advancement and Artificial Intelligence.

The research design used for this dissertation may be used for future research, which could test UK neo-mercantilism post-Brexit or in other EU member states. It could also be used for testing the effects of neo-mercantilism in EU member-states from accession or for comparative studies between member states and for testing neo-mercantilism in other countries or trading blocs around the world, where similar international trade policies that have proved to be largely beneficial have been adopted in one form or the other, for the political economies of sovereign nation states.

6. Appendix 1

Dissertation secondary data set

Year	Trade Openness (%)	Inward FDI Flow ($m)	Outward FDI Flow ($m)	GDP per capita (£)	Balance of Trade (£m)	BoE Interest Rate %	Governing Political Party
1970	41.87	1488	1678	12157	349	7	1
1971	41.53	1771	1988	12580	722	5	1
1972	40.50	1208	2017	13080	-126	9	1
1973	46.22	2723	4981	13902	-1793	13	1
1974	57.23	4374	4376	13555	-4099	11.5	0
1975	51.39	3319	3001	13355	-1715	11.25	0
1976	55.92	3006	4338	13748	-1264	14.25	0
1977	57.38	4427	4173	14093	1197	7	0
1978	53.54	3787	6815	14687	2422	12.5	0
1979	53.23	6469	12539	15219	955	17	1
1980	49.96	10123	11229	14885	5407	14	1
1981	48.08	5879	12153	14762	7602	14.38	1
1982	48.30	5413	7163	15077	5689	10	1
1983	49.48	5179	8184	15706	3299	9.06	1
1984	53.96	-347	7977	16037	131	9.5	1
1985	53.51	5476	10606	16666	4488	11.38	1
1986	49.21	8570	17018	17152	-2090	10.88	1
1987	48.59	15921	28925	18033	-3483	8.38	1

Year	Trade Openness (%)	Inward FDI Flow ($m)	Outward FDI Flow ($m)	GDP per capita (£)	Balance of Trade (£m)	BoE Interest Rate %	Governing Political Party
1988	46.14	22568	41636	19039	-15094	12.88	1
1989	47.42	31650	31378	19476	-18323	14.88	1
1990	47.00	33504	27983	19560	-11117	13.88	1
1991	44.13	16451	23547	19274	-2550	10.38	1
1992	45.10	16559	26151	19294	-4847	6.88	1
1993	48.45	16518	30422	19733	-2658	5.38	1
1994	50.53	10725	43733	20448	-185	6.13	1
1995	50.58	21731	56509	20901	2394	6.38	1
1996	51.85	27390	41714	21383	1604	5.94	1
1997	50.61	37505	74699	21995	3828	7.25	0
1998	48.62	74652	157975	22634	-7910	6.25	0
1999	49.08	89337	242360	23294	-16169	5.5	0
2000	51.83	164130	292047	24083	-20439	6	0
2001	51.96	56091	77412	24645	-26108	4	0
2002	50.57	89761	120902	25128	-32945	4	0
2003	49.64	36011	82074	25881	-30386	3.75	0
2004	44.66	87060	128640	26397	-35397	4.75	0
2005	52.14	252653	159910	26973	-36502	4.5	0
2006	56.04	203636	142255	27460	-36113	5	0
2007	52.34	209515	370395	27936	-39942	5.5	0
2008	56.76	253454	356696	27534	-46189	2	0
2009	54.72	14547	-48398	26158	-34355	0.5	0
2010	59.22	66735	54407	26447	-42593	0.25	1
2011	62.71	27012	80834	26623	-27060	0.25	1
2012	61.83	47651	12024	26794	-37334	0.25	1
2013	61.77	54473	46251	27136	-39238	0.25	1
2014	58.14	71364	-119375	27756	-36223	0.25	1
2015	56.85	58451	-56053	28142	-29788	0.25	1
2016	50.08	299665	41289	28415	-37026	0.25	1

Descriptive Statistics

	N	Range	Minimum	Maximum	Mean	
	Statistic	Statistic	Statistic	Statistic	Statistic	Std. Error
UK Trade Openness %	47	22.21	40.50	62.71	51.2994	.76197
UK Inward FDI Flow	47	300012	-347	299665	52757.13	10945.346
UK Outward FDI Flow	47	489770	-119375	370395	57203.79	13981.322
UK GDP Per Capita	47	16258	12157	28415	20536.87	788.114
UK Balance of Trade	47	53791	-46189	7602	-13637.74	2497.635
BoE Base Interest Rate	47	16.75	.25	17.00	7.2034	.68646
UK Governing party	47	1	0	1	.62	.072
Valid N (listwise)	47					

Std. Deviation	Variance	Skewness		Kurtosis	
Statistic	Statistic	Statistic	Std. Error	Statistic	Std. Error
5.22383	27.288	.189	.347	-.143	.681
75037.514	5630628579.505	2.018	.347	3.300	.681
95851.113	9187435956.171	1.797	.347	3.712	.681
5403.035	29192785.983	.013	.347	-1.505	.681
17122.921	293194424.020	-.503	.347	-1.406	.681
4.70615	22.148	.134	.347	-.892	.681
.491	.241	-.497	.347	-1.832	.681

7. Appendix 2

Homoscedasticity test results and other test results

Run MATRIX procedure:
Macro syntax developed by Ahmad Daryanto

Original Regression model:
Dependent variable
LnTO

R-square
.295

OLS Output

	b	se	t	sig
constant	3.808	.136	28.019	.000
IFDIF	.000	.000	-.707	.483
OFDIF	.000	.000	-1.123	.268
Income	.000	.000	1.240	.222
BoT	.000	.000	-.714	.479
Interest	.000	.005	-.050	.960
Party	-.045	.033	-1.364	.180

------- ANOVA TABLE --------

	SS	df	MS	F	Sig
Model	.141	6.000	.024	2.788	.023
Residual	.338	40.000	.008	-999.000	-999.000

==

Breusch-Pagan and Koenker test

==

The tests use the residuals from the above OLS

OLS output

	b	se	t	sig
constant	5.117	1.702	3.007	.005
IFDIF	.000	.000	-2.076	.044
OFDIF	.000	.000	1.077	.288
Income	.000	.000	-2.505	.016
BoT	.000	.000	-2.835	.007
Interest	-.081	.060	-1.342	.187
Party	-.073	.415	-.175	.862

R-square
.253

------- ANOVA TABLE --------

	SS	df	MS	F	Sig
Model	17.954	6.000	2.992	2.259	.023
Residual	52.983	40.000	1.325	-999.000	-999.000

------- Breusch-Pagan and Koenker test statistics and sig-values --------

	LM	Sig
BP	8.977	.175
Koenker	11.896	.064

Null hypothesis: heteroskedasticity not present (homoskedasticity)

If sig-value less than 0.05, reject the null hypothesis (homoskedasticity)

Note: Breusch-Pagan test is a large sample test and assumes the residuals to be normally distributed

The graph below shows no discernible pattern and provides visual evidence to support homoscedasticity.

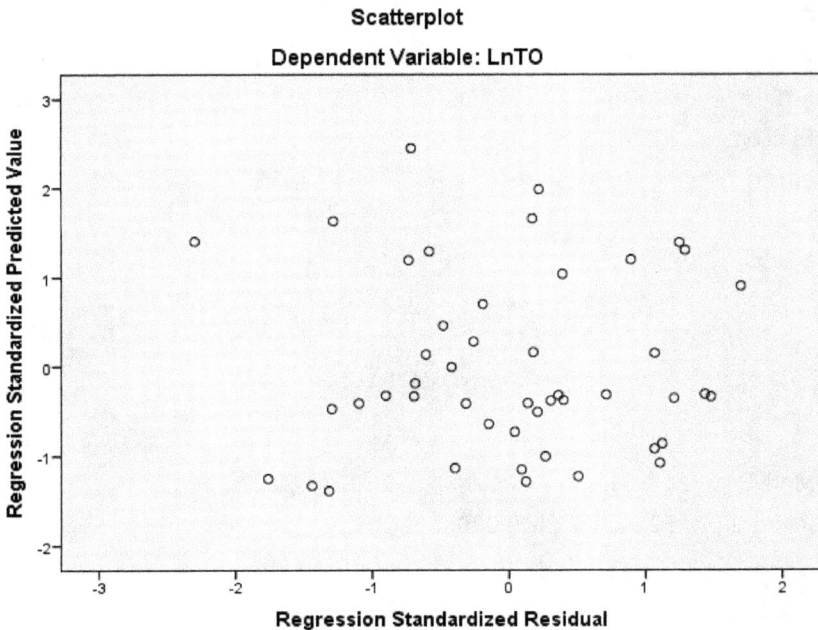

Scatterplot
Dependent Variable: LnTO

AUTOCORRELATION VISUAL TEST (shows no clear pattern)

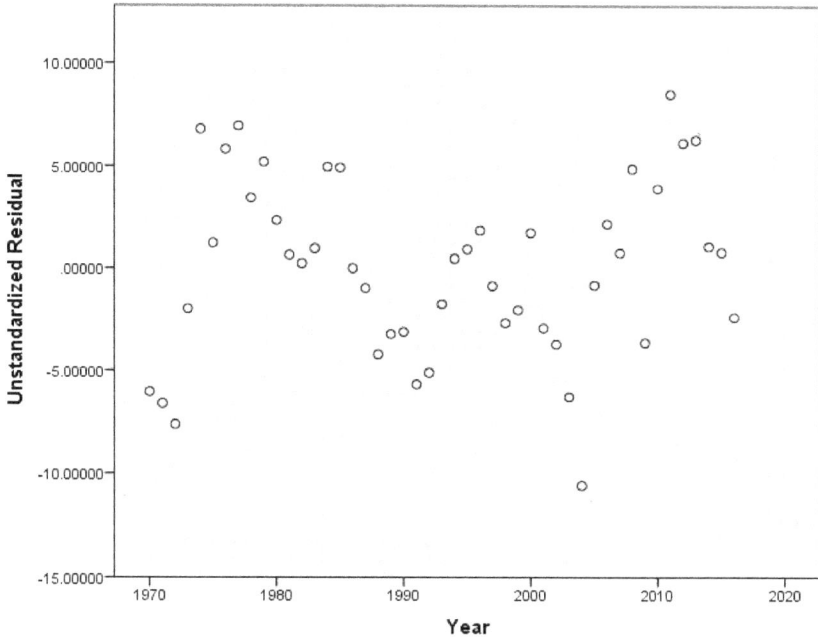

MULTICOLLINEARITY TEST RESULT

Coefficients[a]

Model		Unstandardized Coefficients		Standardized Coefficients			95.0% Confidence Interval for B		Collinearity Statistics	
		B	Std. Error	Beta	t	Sig.	Lower Bound	Upper Bound	Toler-ance	VIF
1	(Constant)	45.788	6.930		6.607	.000	31.793	59.783		
	UK Inward FDI Flow	-1.414E-5	.000	-.203	-.865	.392	.000	.000	.320	3.127
	UK Outward FDI Flow	-6.018E-6	.000	-.110	-.592	.557	.000	.000	.507	1.971
	UK GDP Per Capita	.000	.000	.282	.841	.405	.000	.001	.157	6.361
	UK Balance of Trade	.000	.000	-.357	-1.178	.245	.000	.000	.192	5.212
	BoE Base Interest Rate	-.067	.247	-.060	-.271	.788	-.565	.431	.357	2.799

a. Dependent Variable: UK Trade Openness %

MULTIVARIATE NORMALITY TEST RESULT

Tests of Normality

	Kolmogorov-Smirnov[a]			Shapiro-Wilk		
	Statistic	df	Sig.	Statistic	df	Sig.
UK Inward FDI Flow	.240	47	.000	.689	47	.000
UK Outward FDI Flow	.226	47	.000	.785	47	.000
UK GDP Per Capita	.137	47	.028	.908	47	.001
UK Balance of Trade	.228	47	.000	.855	47	.000
BoE Base Interest Rate	.093	47	.200*	.951	47	.046

8. Appendix 3

Bivariate Correlations

		UK Trade Openness %	UK Inward FDI Flow	UK Outward FDI Flow	UK GDP Per Capita	UK Balance of Trade	BoE Base Interest Rate	UK Governing party
UK Trade Openness %	Pearson Correlation	1	.193	.038	.458**	-.463**	-.422**	-.182
	Sig. (2-tailed)		.194	.801	.001	.001	.003	.222
	N	47	47	47	47	47	47	47
UK Inward FDI Flow	Pearson Correlation	.193	1	.683**	.686**	-.700**	-.466**	-.376**
	Sig. (2-tailed)	.194		.000	.000	.000	.001	.009
	N	47	47	47	47	47	47	47
UK Outward FDI Flow	Pearson Correlation	.038	.683**	1	.443**	-.418**	-.209	-.531**
	Sig. (2-tailed)	.801	.000		.002	.003	.159	.000
	N	47	47	47	47	47	47	47

		UK Trade Openness %	UK Inward FDI Flow	UK Outward FDI Flow	UK GDP Per Capita	UK Balance of Trade	BoE Base Interest Rate	UK Governing party
UK GDP Per Capita	Pearson Correlation	.458**	.686**	.443**	1	-.886**	-.783**	-.245
	Sig. (2-tailed)	.001	.000	.002		.000	.000	.097
	N	47	47	47	47	47	47	47
UK Balance of Trade	Pearson Correlation	-.463**	-.700**	-.418**	-.886**	1	.723**	.301*
	Sig. (2-tailed)	.001	.000	.003	.000		.000	.040
	N	47	47	47	47	47	47	47
BoE Base Interest Rate	Pearson Correlation	-.422**	-.466**	-.209	-.783**	.723**	1	.133
	Sig. (2-tailed)	.003	.001	.159	.000	.000		.372
	N	47	47	47	47	47	47	47
UK Governing party	Pearson Correlation	-.182	-.376**	-.531**	-.245	.301*	.133	1
	Sig. (2-tailed)	.222	.009	.000	.097	.040	.372	
	N	47	47	47	47	47	47	47

**. Correlation is significant at the 0.01 level (2-tailed).*. Correlation is significant at the 0.05 level (2-tailed).

9. Appendix 4

Instructive Interview Transcript

Location: London School of Economics and Political Science
Date: 14th August 2017
Time: 17:00 – 17:30
Dr Thomas Sampson (TS), Interviewee
Adrian Ikeji (AI), Student Researcher & Note taker
Questions and Answers precis (after greeting, introduction and consent form signing)

AI – Is it now imperative for the government to redefine the post-Brexit default negotiation position? Is there a political consensus that no deal is better than a bad deal or the status quo?

TS – I would push back a bit on the idea that there is a consensus between the two major parties at the moment because the literal reading of the manifestos shows that in many ways they were quite similar in that both parties accepted the referendum result and said they want to get the best deal possible for the UK but they were both also willing to leave the single market.

At the same time, the labour party has clearly been hedging its position slightly in that different players in the party have been saying different things about what the party wants to achieve and if we look at the pattern of voting in the general election, at least part of the reason why Labour did better than expected is that it swept up support from arguably pro-Remain voters, which was somewhat surprising but can be explained by the idea that Labour was seen as more likely to pursue a softer Brexit than the Conservatives so I would say there wasn't or certainly it wasn't clear in the public's mind if there is consensus on what the UK wants to get out of Brexit.

The Conservative party for the most part seems to want to pursue a hard Brexit and by that I mean leaving the single market and the customs union and there are elements within the Labour party that agree with that but it appears that there are other elements that would like to stay within it so it is not quite clear what their position is regardless of the similarities in the manifestos at the last general election. The split in the Labour party on this issue is much deeper but they have been able to use ambiguity quite successfully, so far.

AI – So do you think at this point in time it's important for the current government to express what the default negotiation position is to the wider populace?

TS – Yes, I would agree to that in that I think, clearly Britain is quite split on the whole issue - it was a narrowly won referendum – it wasn't clear what the referendum would mean and there hasn't been a coming together since the referendum. I think the country is as split now as it was a year ago, so if the government is going to get a broad consensus within the population for whatever Brexit ends up meaning, I think it still needs to explain to people what it is trying to achieve – why it is trying to achieve that and how it is going to achieve that.

So far I think if you look back to the PM's Lancaster House speech earlier this year, that set out quite clearly what she would like to achieve but it was a little bit less clear about how it would achieve it or even why those should be the goals that we aimed for and I think the consequence of that was that there wasn't widespread support for that position which is not to say that there was a majority opposition to it but just that it was a position that was relatively popular with Leave voters but relatively unpopular with Remain voters.

And we then had the general elections which the PM called, at least in part to try to achieve a mandate for that position and now with the hung parliament outcome it would be hard to argue that she received a clear mandate for that position so I think the Conservatives still have work to do to develop a consensus and support for their position and I think that is still work in progress.

AI – Thank you very much for that detailed answer. Now moving on to my next question, what is your understanding of what happens if no New-Deal is agreed with the EU or if we just walk away from negotiations? Should it mean continued Single Market Membership with Customs Union concessions, immigration concessions and payments? Or WTO rules (as indicated in the Article 50 letter), with no defined government yearly payment to the EU but new costs for market access to businesses?

TS – What would happen if we don't have any deal before or by the end of March 2019, we leave without any kind of deal - from a Trade perspective that would mean that we would then trade with the EU broadly speaking under similar terms as those with which we currently trade with countries like the USA or China which is to say under WTO terms.

That would mean there would be new tariffs on Trade with the EU and it would also mean an increase in non-tariff barriers between the UK and the EU so if things like the passporting rights that allow financial services firms to operate throughout the EU, those would disappear so it would be harder for those firms to export their services.

So what I would expect to see would be a contraction in Trade with the EU, which would reduce and have a negative effect on the UK economy relative to whatever would have happened in the alternative scenario and therefore it would leave the UK worse off than it would otherwise have been.

AI – Would you say it was at all possible that in the event that negotiations fail we could continue trading relations with the EU under the status quo?

TS - No I would say that if we don't get a deal and we don't withdraw our Article 50 notification, and there's a legal question regarding whether we even can withdraw it, then my understanding is that the default would be at the end of March 2019 for the UK to leave the EU and from that date we lose all the privileges and Trading rights from being a member of the European Union.

AI – Excuse me Dr. Sampson,but would that also mean that all the Preferential Trade Agreements that were negotiated by the EU on behalf of the UK while it was a member of the single market, would have to be re-negotiated by the UK?

TS – Yes. Now how exactly that process would work is unclear because there isn't any precedent for this happening. My hope and to some extent expectation is that as long as there is goodwill on both sides, it would be relatively straight forward for the UK to get a deal with those countries that kind of essentially maintains the status quo of those relationships but that would be contingent on the other Trading partner, so for example South Korea is a good example of a country that the EU has a Free-Trading Agreement with; it would require South Korea's agreement to allow the UK to continue trading with it on those preferential terms and that will require some diplomatic work to get and may require some concessions from the UK.

AI – Thank you for that. My next question is how does unilateral tariff liberalisation compare with a comprehensive Free-Trade Agreement; broadly speaking positively or negatively? Why?

TS – We did some quantitative studies of that here at the LSE and we found that if the UK leaves the EU without any kind of new agreement that would lead to a fall in UK living standards.

If on top of that, the UK unilaterally liberalises Trade, which is to say it cuts all its tariffs on Trade with the EU and the rest of the world, that makes the UK better off than it would be with no deal but still worse off than it would be if it remained in the EU.

So what our research suggests is that unilateral liberalisation can partly off-set the cost of Brexit but it can't fully off-set the cost. And the reason basically is that, part of the benefits of Trade liberalisation is that you reduce the cost of imports but part of the benefit is that you also create new export opportunities for your firms and unilateral liberalisations does one of those things which is it cuts import costs but not the other.

AI – Is an early Transitional Agreement with the EU better for businesses than the certainty of an early no-deal? Why?

TS – That's a good question. The way I think about this is: if you think about what businesses are worried about here, there are two aspects to it.

First, businesses don't like uncertainty because it makes it hard for them to plan and that might mean that they delay investments and that reduces output.

The other thing is that we are not just facing uncertainty here, but we're facing actual new costs so even if they were certain that we were going to leave the EU with no deal that would still be a problem for business because that would mean that they would be facing new Trade costs which would make it harder for them to trade with the rest of the EU and is bad for business. So those are two negative effects on businesses.

The certainty of an early no-deal solves the uncertainty problem but it doesn't solve the new costs problem. Whereas a transitional Agreement, at least temporarily solves the problem of facing higher trade costs, if you assume that the transitional Agreement is something like the status quo but it also means that you don't fully resolve the uncertainty because you're effectively just saying you push the uncertainty down the road.

It kind of depends which of those components of the problems businesses are facing or which is more important to the business and at least in the short-run I am not sure what the answer to that would be.

In the long-run I would probably say that the problem of higher Trade barriers would be more problematic but in the short-run it is more difficult to predict.

AI – Would it be fair to say that you see both scenarios as problems rather than solutions or opportunities?

TS – Yes. They're not really solutions.

AI – Lastly, of the three statistically significant findings from my quantitative research presented in the information sheet, which may be the most crucial indicator or relationship worth monitoring post-Brexit?

TS – I think the link between Trade Openness and Income per capita is important and I see the relationship you have identified in your research.

The finding that countries that are more open for Trade tend to have higher Income per capita is backed by a large body of both theoretical and empirical evidence to support the fact that as countries become more open it has positive effects on Income per capita and I think that is a useful frame for thinking about what the effects of Brexit are likely to be, in the sense that if the UK does close itself off and trades less with the rest of the world that will have negative income effects so I think that's a useful result for thinking about the likely economic effects of Brexit.

AI – But if the government were to take decisions within the economy that lead to a rise in GDP per capita that also has a positive effect on Trade Openness as demand for imports increases so there is bi-directional causation, isn't there?

TS - I agree there is a two way relationship. The reason I stress the relationship from Openness to GDP per capita is that I would see Openness not as a goal in itself from an economics perspective, but as a means to an end.

What we care about in the end is welfare and living standards, Income per capita doesn't perfectly capture that but it is a useful proxy for thinking about it. Whereas, Trade Openness per se, I wouldn't care about Trade Openness unless it is affecting living standards so that's why I stress that side of the relationship.

Interview concluded at 17:25 (with thanks and a commitment to supply transcripts for review and final consent within two weeks).

Pro-Business Sample Interview

Dissertation Interview Transcript
Location: Birkbeck, University of London
Date: 24th August 2017
Time: 17:20 – 17:50
Prof Klaus Nielsen (KN), Interviewee
Adrian Ikeji (AI), Student Researcher & Note taker
Questions and Answers precis (after greeting, introduction and consent form signing)

AI – The background to this first question is the UK General Election Result of June 2017 so my question is: Is it now imperative for the UK government to redefine the post-Brexit default negotiation position? Is there a political consensus that no deal is better than a bad deal or the status quo?

KN – I think this is something that is very difficult to answer because there are many conflicting messages from different members of the government and also from different members of the Labour Party so to give a coherent answer to this question is almost practically impossible.

You have the current Chancellor of the Exchequer who is interested in a long transitional period with as few limitations to free trade as possible and then you have a very radical wing of the Conservative Party around the International Trade Secretary and some of the more hard-core euro-sceptics, who give completely different voices here; you find very rarely that there are sort of joint media briefings or messages like we saw the other day when Chancellor Hammond and Dr Fox shared a platform to launch a joint statement.

I think it is a very confusing situation and honestly, if one is looking for leadership from the Prime Minister at the present time, it seems to be non-existent. She appears to be silent on this matter so I think it is still very uncertain what the position actually is.

Also I would say that with the Labour Party, you're quite right that they were also clear in their manifesto and they acknowledged the will of the majority from the Brexit referendum about leaving the single market and customs union but there are still quite powerful voices inside the party who are in favour of a softer Brexit which does not involve giving up membership of the EU single market etc.

The kind of government negotiating position unveiled last week at the launch of the customs union position paper which aims to achieve an arrangement that is in practice a customs union in all but name just muddies the water further. Honestly I don't think a clear answer is possible.

AI – What if we consider the clear objectives set out in the government's Article 50 letter to the EU Commission which triggered this period of negotiations, would you agree that there is a need for that consensus and its ramifications to be better explained to the country?

KN – Yes, I think so. Let me also say in response to the question about the original position of no deal being better than a bad deal that it is true that in that sense, there has been a development. It is not something the government is saying anymore and in practice they appear to have moved away from that position and they are trying to make the best deal with the EU possible.

However, I still think there are fringe members of the Conservative Party who seriously think that the position is unchanged and that may influence the government's negotiation position because they will be furious if there is any kind of modification to the objectives, although there has been some minor concessions by the Brexit Secretary already on the order of negotiations. I think the position of the government is pretty unclear because they still have very vague and generalised principles that cannot be sustained. It is impossible to say that after March 2019 that the European Court of Justice, for example, would have no say because there has never been any signal from the other side that they could accept any kind of tailor made court or arbitrator to deal with the many issues raised by Brexit.

I think there certainly needs to be more clarity and details and I accept that in negotiations it could be self-defeating to start out with too many details which may be part of the UK rationale but all indications at the moment suggest that there is a lot more work for the government to do.

AI – Thank you very much for that detailed answer. Now moving on to my next question, what is your understanding of what happens if no New-Deal is agreed with the EU or if we just walk away from negotiations? Should it mean continued Single Market Membership with Customs Union concessions, immigration concessions and payments? Or WTO rules (as indicated in the Article 50 letter), with no defined government yearly payment to the EU but new costs for market access to businesses?

KN – I think it will certainly be WTO rules, there's no doubt about it. I think it would be unrealistic and pure fantasy to think that the EU would accept anything like the status quo with the UK opting to leave.

I think the argument that something like the status quo may be possible is that it is in the economic interest of EU car-makers in Germany for example, to continue as much free trade in the UK market as possible, and it's true there are some economic arguments but in that sense and many others, the EU is a political unit so it is unthinkable that they will compromise on the overall foundation principles of the EU in order to accommodate these kinds of economic interests.

So for me, I think it is more likely to be WTO rules for the UK and there is also the economic interests of the remaining member states like France and others keen to attract some of the services businesses away from the UK and also the risk of other countries like Denmark, Netherlands and some of the A8 countries wanting a similar deal as the UK, if it gets a great deal, so I think both sides will have to accept the costs and problems of the barriers to trade that seem inevitable for political reasons as the political interests are strong.

AI – Just to be clear, are you suggesting that the UK's only way of maintaining the status quo in relation to trading arrangements is if the Article 50 notification is retracted?

KN – Yes, unless there is an agreement of some sort. I was at a meeting with labour parties in Europe recently and one member of the parliament (MEP) from the Republic of Ireland said well in principle it would be difficult to retract it formally but where there is the political will then a way could be found. There are some very clever lawyers in the EU Commission so they'll probably find a way.

The important issue is whether there is the political will, and I'm not sure that all the 27 member states will be happy to accept a retraction. Of course if the larger member states are agreeable to the idea then there will be a lot of pressure on the less influential members not to curtail the existing relationship with the UK. A lot of things will have to happen in the next year for this outcome to be realised.

AI – Thank you for that. I'm looking forward to your next answer because of your economics background and knowledge of the business environment in the EU and UK, so my next question is how does unilateral tariff liberalisation for the UK outside the EU compare with a comprehensive free trade agreement with the EU; broadly speaking positively or negatively? Why?

KN – I think the comprehensive Free-Trade deal with the EU is more attractive and it's quite obvious it should be in the short-run, disregarding the difficulties of achieving this, if you consider the share of current Trade with the EU, even though it is declining it is still by far the most important part of UK Trade.

And then we can think of how realistic it would be to liberalise Trade or reach a Free-Trade Agreement with parts of the rest of the world. The first country on the list would be the USA and you will recall what happened when the International Trade Secretary went there recently with his broad ideas of trade deals and extreme deregulation. He ruined the whole purpose of his trip by getting drawn into talking about chlorinated chicken products and raising more questions than answers.

There are many issues in the relationship between the EU and the US, from genetically modified organisms, hormone beef etc. and the problem here is that, is it in the EU's interest regarding the relationship with the US? Are they different from the interests of the UK with the US? It might be different in some respects but in most respects, I think they are the same as what the UK would do outside the EU and would be to instil most of the standards and regulations the EU already has, because there is likely to be a majority opinion in support of this. So there may not be much to be gained by the unilateral liberalisation option.

Also think about the amount of time it takes to negotiate Free-Trade Agreements, they take ages even when they are expected to be easy, and they often have a lot of exemptions. I just think if one looks at the reality, completely free trade is a phantom and cannot be experienced.

Free-trade is one thing, the Customs Union is another and the single market is the third thing.

The single market where you have no differences in regulations; no controls and internal borders and mutual recognition of standards and so on is something I could not really understand from the UK Brexit debates. They seem to think that the EU is a Free-Trade Agreement and only a few people seem to understand that it is a single market and how important that is. That explains partly why the EU is so important for the UK and that will not be achieved by a Free-Trade Agreement.

AI – Is an early Transitional Agreement with the EU better for businesses than the certainty of an early no-deal? Why?

KN – I recently listened to a presentation by the Chairwoman of the Confederation of British Industry and she put it quite clearly that the interest of business is to have something which comes as close to the single market as possible. Point two is to have a long transitional period, and point three as few restrictions as possible in terms of employing the skills we need.

I think it's clear that a cliff edge exit in 2019 would be a disaster for businesses even if it would then force them to make adjustments but adjustments are unlikely to happen that quickly. I would think one thing that is happening now in this uncertain situation is that a lot of Banking Institutions are making moves to try to pre-empt the loss of passporting rights by creating affiliations there, so some things are happening even though the situation is not clear and it's obvious that if the situation became clear then even more business decisions would be taken. However, for businesses where their supply chains are very integrated especially because of the benefits of the single market, the consequences of a cliff edge or no deal would be catastrophic so I think an early transitional agreement is more desirable for businesses.

AI – Lastly, of the three statistically significant findings from my quantitative research presented in the information sheet, which may be the most crucial indicator or relationship worth monitoring post-Brexit to assess the impact it is having on the economy?

TS – I think it is quite obvious that the second relationship identified between GDP per capita and Trade Openness is important but it is also obvious that it is very difficult to identify to what extent those changes in the independent variable is an effect caused by the Brexit decision.

So to the extent that Brexit has an identifiable effect on GDP per capita and a corresponding effect on UK Trade Openness, then I think that that relationship of the three is the most important one.

Also, Interest rates in the UK depends largely on economic growth and economic policy in general in the UK compared to other countries, it could be also that there are some kinds of international trends that mean that Interest rates generally increase as it did in the 1980s and so on and not just about what is happening in the domestic economy.

AI – But we are looking at this from the angle where the government may need to take decisions or intervene within the economy to mitigate or counteract negative effects of Brexit, aren't we? If we look back to the period just after the Brexit referendum last year, we may recall that one of the first measures taken by the Governor of the Bank of England was to cut Interest rates and some may argue that those actions stabilised the economy to some extent since then and post-Brexit the relationship between Interest rates and openness may suggest that further cuts to the current rate may be likely if the consequences of Brexit are as severe as some experts are predicting.

KN – Interest rates are also affected by the currency exchange rate and that has seen a significant adjustment since the Brexit referendum certainly and that affects the attractiveness of the economy for investment and financial movements.

I think the important relationship is with GDP per capita because it is important for employment, welfare, tax revenue etc. and so in that sense all other factors are contributory factors. If you have growth there are far more opportunities. Therefore if you pay a price in terms of lower growth then it will be felt in many other respects.

Interview concluded at 17:50 (with thanks and a commitment to supply transcripts for review and final consent within two weeks).

10. References

Apergis, N. (2009). Foreign Direct Investment Inward and Outward: Evidence from panel data, developed and developing economies, and open and closed economies. The American Economist.54 (2), p21-27.

Brannen, J. (1992). Considerations using multi-methods. In: Brannen, J Mixing Methods: Qualitative and Quantitative Research. Hampshire: Avebury. p3-33.

Babones, S. (2007). Trade Globalization, Economic Development, and the Income Stratification Process. Available: http://hdl.handle.net/21 23/8056. Last accessed 1st Feb 2017.

Baccaro, L. (2011). Labor, Globalization and Inequality. In: Brady, D Comparing European Workers Part B: Policies and Institutions. Bingly: Emerald Group Publishing. p231.

Bello, W (2004). Deglobalization: Ideas for a New World Economy. London: Zed Books Ltd. p1-118.

Cooper, R. (1986). Macroeconomics in an Open Economy.Science - American Association for the Advancement of Science.233 (4769), p1155-1156.

Daryanto, A. (2013). Heteroskedasticity Subroutine for SPSS. Available: https://sites.google.com/site/ahmaddaryanto/scripts/Heterogeneity-test. Last accessed 28th July 2017.

Dinu, Vasile and Dabija, D. (2015). Economic Deglobalization: From Hypothesis to reality. E a M: Ekonomie a Management. XVIII (2), p4-13.

Dhingra, S and Sampson, T. (2016). Life after Brexit: What are the UK's options outside the European Union? Centre for Economic Performance - LSE. 1 (1), p1-12.

Ekholm, K. and Sodersten, B. (2002).Growth and Trade vs Trade and Growth.Small Business Economics.19 (2), p147-162.

Forte, R. and Moura, R. (2013). The Effects of Foreign Direct Investment on the Host Country's Economic Growth: Theory and Empirical Evidence. The Singapore Economic Review.58 (3), p1-24.

Frankel, J.A and Romer, D. (1999). Does Trade Cause Growth? The American Economic Review.89 (3), p379-399.

Gries, T and Redlin, M. (2012). Trade Openness and Economic Growth: A Panel Causality Analysis. International Conferences of RCIE, KIET, and APEA.1 (1), P16-18.

Guerrieri, P and Padoan, P. (1986).Neomercantilism and international economic stability.International Organization.40 (1), p29-42.

Gylfason, T. (1993).Optimal Savings, Interest Rates and Endogenous Growth.The Scandinavian Journal of Economics.95 (4), p517-533.

Hager, W. (1987).The NeomercantilistConstraint.The annals of the American Academy of Political and Social Science.492 (1), p61-68.

Harvey, C. (1991). Interest Rate Based Forecasts of German Economic Growth. WeltwirtschaftlichesArchiv.127 (4), p701-718.

Hill, C.W.L. (2014). Globalization. In: Hooper, P. International Business: Competing in the Global Marketplace. 10th ed. Maidenhead: McGraw-Hill Education. p5-24, 180-183.

Johnson, H.G. (1974). Mercantilism: Past, Present, Future (Presidential Address). In: Johnson, H.G. The New Mercantilism. Oxford: Basil Blackwell. p1-19.

Kim, D. and Lin, S. (2009). Trade and Growth at Different Stages of Economic Development. Journal of Development Studies.45 (8), p1211-1224.

Krueger, A.O. (1987). Protectionism and Non-Tariff barriers in World Trade. Harvard International Review.9 (3), p19-23.

Li, X. and Liu, X. (2005). Foreign Direct Investment and Economic Growth: An Increasingly Endogenous Relationship. World Development.33 (3), p393-407.

May, T. (2017). Prime Minister's letter to Donald Tusk triggering Article 50. Available: https://www.gov.uk/government/uploads/system/uploads/attachment_data/file/604079/Prime_Ministers_letter_to_European_Council_President_Donald_Tusk.pdf. Last accessed 28th August 2017.

May, T. (2017). The government's negotiating objectives for exiting the EU: PM speech. Available: https://www.gov.uk/government/speeches/the-governments-negotiating-objectives-for-exiting-the-eu-pm-speech. Last accessed 28th August 2017.

McFadzean, F. (1972). Towards an Open World Economy. London: The Macmillan Press Ltd. p219.

Rallings, C and Thrasher, M. (2016).BRITISH ELECTORAL FACTS 1832 - 2006. 7th ed. Oxford: Routledge. p59.

Raza, W. (2007). European Union Trade Politics: Pursuit of Neo-Mercantilism in different fora? In: Blaas, W. and Becker, J. Strategic Arena Switching in International Trade Arena. Hampshire: Ashgate Publishing Limited. p67-96.

Ritzer, G. (2007). The Blackwell Companion to Globalization. Oxford: Blackwell Publishing. p10 - 150.

Thirlwall, A.P. and Gibson, H.D. (1992). Balance of Payments Theory and the United Kingdom Experience. 4th ed. London: Macmillan. p341-350.

Trade Analysis Branch (2016). Key Indicators and Trends in International Trade. 4th ed. Geneva: UNCTAD. p9-28.

Wacziarg, R. (2001). Measuring the Dynamic Gains from Trade. The World Bank Economic Review.15 (3), p393-429.

Yin, R.K. (2014). Case Study Research Design and Methods. 5th ed. London: SAGE Publications, Inc. p45-56.

Wang, C., Liu, X. and Wei, Y. (2004). Impact of openness on growth in different country groups. The World Economy.27 (4), p567-585.

PAPER 2

Report Title: Rent-seeking; an obstacle to development or an engine for development?

A discussion report by Adrian Ikeji

Date: 08/12/2016

Word count: 4158

Introduction

Rent-seeking is a pervasive and widely studied economic phenomenon that has been quantitatively researched since the nineteen sixties but has been taking place for hundreds of years, arguably since the dawn of commerce itself and has taken many forms over time.

Over the years, Rent-seeking applications have been observed and chronicled by economists in the following broad areas, as outlined by Congleton, Hillman and Konrad (2008): Regulation of industry, protectionist rent-seeking, soft budgets and moral hazard, rent-seeking in the context of economic development, the relationship between rent-seeking and economic growth, rent-seeking inside the firm, rent-seeking between insiders and outsiders, office seeking and rent creation in democratic politics, litigation, history and civil society, public sector non-jobs and welfare-seeking. Most of which have direct and indirect ramifications on an economy with varying degrees of significance.

In this essay however, I will be focusing on the aspects of rent-seeking that highlight some consequences, potential benefits and policy frameworks that may aid economic development as can be measured by Gross National Product (GNP) per capita rather than any other form of quantifiable development such as population growth, consumption per capita, infrasture development, structure of labour force, social conditions or unfreedoms (literacy rate, life expectancy, health care quality, infant mortality) etc. principally because of the word-count constraint for this academic exercise and the scope of the module.

I will begin by setting out a comprehensive perspective of the nature and classification of rent-seeking activities before addressing the substantive research questions that flow from the topic i.e. What makes rent-seeking a problem for development?; What makes it helpful?; The ways to choose only the helpful aspects to drive the engine of development. This essay will not be addressing the political considerations or ramifications of economic policy and neither will it attempt to present otherwise relevant work on Public Choice Theory or Game Theory because of the afforementioned constraints.

Perspectives and Definitions:

In Adam Smith's seminal book, "The Wealth of Nations Vol 1", first published in 1776, he distinguishes between the sources of national income and defines the sources classically as follows: Wages as compensation for labour; Rent as a price determined bounty of nature and Profit as payment to the capitalist for provision of factors of production i.e. financial gain for the business person after deducting the costs of doing business. In the same book he describes the motivation behind entrepreneurial effort by stating (Book I Chapter II page 1), *"It is not from the benevolence of the butcher, the brewer, or the baker that we expect our dinner, but from their regard to their own self-interest. "* .

Smith's (1776) observation 240 years ago was echoed by Buchanan and Tullock (1962) when they concluded that public interest is an aggregation of private decision-makers motivated by self-interest. Ergo people's actions in the economic and political marketplaces are motivated by self-interest which leads to Pareto Optimality or efficiency which does not necessarily lead to a socially desirable allocation of resources or economic growth or development, for that matter. I believe structural checks and balances are required to guarantee desirable outcomes in the public interest and I will expatiate some pertinent policies in the course of this essay.

In modern terms, wages may be defined as a contractual payment for the use of land, property, labour or service.

Economic Rent (also known as scarcity value or prize or monopoly rent or scarcity premium) is a generic term used to describe: Income from any factor of production (Land, Labour, capital etc.) above and beyond what is needed to keep that factor employed at its current level i.e. the incomes/costs that would not exist in a perfect market.

Tullock (1967) identified the idea of inefficiencies (rent costs, the invention of rent-seeking) as consequences of income/wealth transfers in society. He postulated the following:

1. The transfers themselves cost society nothing but the resources/activities used to encourage or resist the policies are costly.

2. The social cost is similar to the cost of theft in its unproductive and redistributive sense, while profits are productive and create new wealth.

I must point out that economic rents and profits are legal proceeds of endeavour and there is no distinction made between the two in accountancy and taxation either.

Rent-seeking is a term coined by Krueger (1974). It could be defined as unproductive entrepreneurship or pursuing additional financial benefits for non-productive activities i.e. without creating any new wealth by taking advantage of monopolies to maximise financial reward. She incorrectly presumed, at the time, that rents would attract resources of equal value (complete dissipation presumption) and the value of resources used is usually not observable, according to Krueger.

Tullock (1980) developed the Contest Success Function/lottery model which better estimates the value of resources lost in the pursuit of monopoly rents because losses increase as contenders increase. He postulates that rent-seeking is often carried out by influencing public policy for personal financial gain and the Wealth Dilemma leads to a rational decision to rent-seek when faced with the choice between risking capital to increase productivity or increase wealth by rent-seeking without risking capital. It is argued that rent-seeking is beneficial to the winning firm but often a pure loss to the economy as a whole.

Rent-seeking leads to wealth redistribution (from taxpayers to special interest groups) rather than an increase in economic productivity or growth.

According to the World Development Report (1987), rent-seeking encompasses lobbying activities devised to capture the rents i.e. scarcity premiums that are attached to licenses and quotas e.g. lobbies that aim to secure import licenses in trade and payment regimes that rely on exchange and import controls (in developing countries) and also industrial licenses, public purchasing and import quotas. The same report describes rent-seeking as constituting part of Directly Unproductive Profit-seeking (DUP) activities which also includes policy interventions that create rents.

Rent-seeking may be distinguished from normal entrepreneurial profit-seeking because the latter is a consensual transfer of wealth in a win – win transaction as opposed to the coercive transfer of wealth that characterises the former.

CLASSIFICATIONS AND EXAMPLES

Classifications and Examples

Rent-seeking activities and other DUP activities may be categorized based on the prevailing market conditions and the effect of activity on the market according to Bhagwati (1982). His taxonomy may be summarised as follows:

Type 1: Free markets that remain free through intervention, e.g. Zero-tariff outcome lobbying activities such as the pressure and business tactics exerted by a) lobby groups representing the Pharmaceutical industry keen to maximise the rents of their intellectual property rights (and often overcharging public health organisations such as the NHS). b) Food and drink manufacturers threatened by sugar taxes. c) Tobacco Industry lobbies threatened by increasing public health awareness and taxation insensitivity. d) The automobile industry threatened by the cost of eco-friendly policy innovation and environmental health standards. e) Antitrust disputing enterprises incentivised by quantums and unproductive contractual damages. f) Greenmailing activities by corporate bandits and short-selling speculation of arbitrageurs in commodity, futures and equity markets.

Type 2: Free markets that become distorted, e.g. a) Monopoly seeking activities such as the activities of the Banking Industry lobby groups which cost the United Kingdom (UK) government c£850 Billion in bailout packages which significantly increased the per capita debt burden on the citizenry and reduced the choices available to entrepreneurs and other banking customers at the same time as bonus culture in the Banking industry persisted and lending waned. b) The Buy to leave phenomenon in the UK housing market whereby foreign investors commodify London property units as a vehicle to generate capital gains only, with the properties being unavailable to the rental market restricting supply and pressurising property prices making rental affordability and ownership more and more fraught for the resident citizenry. c) Tariff seeking (and tariff evasion) activities such as grease payments in developing countries, and illegal activities such as smuggling, counterfeiting, bribery and other forms of corrupt practices.

Type 3: Initially distorted markets that become free markets, e.g. a) Tariff removing lobbying such as exporters, domestic manufacturers and producers lobbying for the relaxation quantitative restrictions and removal of duties that hinder export growth and reallocation of resources to areas of the economy where comparative advantages exist. b) Strategic privatisation activities/ policies such as transferring land rights, selling off state infrastructure and organisations and targeted subsidies to pick economic winners in a state coordinated effort to kick-start and accelerate growth and economic development.

Type 4: Situations where markets are initially distorted and remain distorted, e.g. a) License seeking activities of cartel-like groups seeking to limit or frustrate competition such as the Black taxis in London threatened by competition from private hire operators and innovative technologies introduced by UBER and Addison Lee for instance. b) Revenue seeking activities of state and enterprises such as politically driven increases in taxation rates, business reaction to changes in legislation and bureaucratic delays and costs etc.

I must state that there is a debate to be had around the accuracy or reasonableness of the presumptions made in order to describe and categorise prevailing market conditions and hence the types of rent-seeking activities covered above, as the intial market conditions are more idealistic and theoretical than realistic and the impacts of activities and interventions create a range of distortions or variations which may not be readily quantified or observed empirically.

Common Conditions That Encourage Rent-Seeking Activities

The conditions that promote adverse rent-seeking activities may typically include any or a combination of the following:

a) Weak property rights e.g where entrepreneurs can make more gains by trying to appropriate stores of wealth than by participating in productive economic activities directly.

b) The Payoffs provided by state policies for certain activities.

c) Unstable incentive systems for productive activities.

d) Bureaucracies that hinder rather than help economic developmental activities.

e) Corruption and a lack of public accountability and transparency mechanisms.

f) Weak or non-existent social infrastructure and civil society organisation.

g) Risks to investment and lack of state protection.

h) Litigiousness of society/culture.

i) Predatory State.

Rent-Seeking Entrepreneurship

According to Baumol (1990), at times entrepreneurs may operate like parasites by actually damaging the economy. The way an entrepreneur conducts business affairs at a particular point in time or phase of the enterprise depends on the reward structure in the economy or rules of the game, as he puts it. Entrepreneurs are ingenious and creative in finding ways that add to their own wealth, power, and prestige and are not partcularly concerned if activity is productive. Therefore, entrepreneurial activity could be productive, innovative, unproductive or rent-seeking and even criminal.

From a historical perspective, he refers to entrepreneurial activities such as enterprising use of the legal system, plundering backed by military activity, quests for grants of land and patents of monopoly from the sovereign leader etc. which may actually contribute to production in cases where the recipient of land given by the monarch, uses it more efficiently than the previous owner did, for instance.

He also identifies some modern threats to productive entrepreneuship including litigation, corporate takeovers, tax evasion and tax avoidance efforts. High tax rates also make it difficult for entrepreneurs to make profits through productive means.

Policy suggestions of note include a) Changes to taxation policies on assets i.e. having higher rates of capital gains tax for assets held for shorter periods and reduced rates for longer periods. b) Deregulation of transport service provision such as in the Airlines and Railways industries. c) Instituting fair trade commisions like in Japan, for instance, to reduce antitrust litigiousness.

The underlying theme of hints from Baumol's work in relation to development policy is the fact that the structure of rewards in society, created by government, influences the activities of entrepreneurs without altering the ultimate profit-seeking goals.

Rentier States, Developmental States and Policies

Moore (2004) gives a comprehensive description of the rentier state characterised by natural resource rents in the control of central government and big companies from crude oil and economically significant deposits of geological minerals, strategic rents (foreign development aid, military assistance, access tolls etc.) which are hard to quantify and have unclear consequences for economic growth at best, weak ties with domestic civil society groups, and poor organisational and political capabilities.

The rentier state evolves as a by-product of globalisation and the bipolar world of economically unequal countries (rich and poor) however, it is argued that governments of such states may be able to generate more reliable revenue streams by taxing labour incomes more efficiently and reducing capital gains taxes on assets, similar to Baumol's proposition, but as a governance dividend which will enhance the tax paying culture, improve political ties with society, incentivise capitalist investors within the state and lead to economic growth.

The lessons from the economic development success story of the United States of America (USA) in the nineteenth century when it became the world's leading mineral producing and manufacturing country, analysed by David and Wright (1997), are that large scale mobilisation of human resources and the application of new technologies were pivotal in creating a positive developmental feedback cycle which spurred on productivity, although the perception of natural resource abundance and technological superiority may have been socially constructed. Generous rewards under Mineral Laws, liberal exploration policies and generous private property rights encouraged prospecting activities which led to an expansion of natural resource output coupled with an ongoing process of learning, investment injection, technological progress and cost reduction which transformed a perception of resource abundance into an engine for national development.

Evans (1995) explores the stark contrasts between predatory and developmental states with a view to sign-posting transformational road maps or blueprints for economic growth. He cites Zaire (today known as the Democratic Republic of Congo – a Natural Resource rich country then and now) under the late President Mobutu Seseseko, as an archetypal case of the former, and describes the state as extracting stupendous amounts of the otherwise investible surplus (economic rents) while providing little or nothing in the way of collective goods in return and thereby impeding economic and developmental transformation. The predatory state creates the ideal conditions for neo-utilitarian rent-seeking activities where paying for rights is common practice and everything is for sale. I am inclined to add many more countries in sub-saharan Africa to form a list of predatory states, with Nigeria (with all its squandered and misappropriated rents and untapped growth potential) at the top of any such list because of its undeniable historical parallels with Zaire.

Developmental states on the other hand, foster long-term entrepreneurial perspectives among the private elites by increasing incentives to engage in transformative investments and lowering the risks. Evans (1995, p.44) referring to developmental states, states that, "*On balance, the consequences of their actions promote rather than hinder transformation.*" He cites the East Asian newly industrialised countries (NICs) of the 1980s, Taiwan and South Korea as states worth emulating by other developing countries seeking economic transformation; He charts their developmental stories and highlights some instumental policies from which I gleaned the following:

1. It is imperative to formulate collective goals with societal ties instead of allowing office-holders to pursue their individual interests. This could be seen as the test for embedded autonomy of state.

2. The state must institute coherent and competent bureacratic organisations to administer development and stimulate growth.

3. Clientelistic ties (bungs, kick-backs and patronage culture) with big business interest groups must be avoided to reduce rent-seeking activities.

4. State owned enterprises (SOEs) can be a key instrument in industrial development as Taiwan has demonstrated (and China more recently, although the Chinese model may not lead to political freedom).

5. The secret of the developmental state lies in the combination of autonomy (capability of formulating its own goals and trusting agents implicitly to follow through/deliver) and societal embeddedness (strong social ties in surrounding society).

I believe that, in an extension to the neo-hobbesian appropriability theory espoused by Mayshar, Moav, Neeman and Pascali (2015, p.48) which attributes an efficient and protective responsibility on the state against appropriation so that citizens can be taxed, I would argue that the developmental state has the responsibility to protect the citizenry from misappropriation of public funds/wealth which creates an urgent need to improve institutional quality and tackle corruption transparently and robustly in society.

Overcoming the Natural Resource Curse

According to Sachs and Warner (2001), most current explanations for the curse have a crowding out rationality which is described as the activities linked to the abundance of natural resources stifling out other activities that could create growth and concluding curiously that natural resources harm growth. The activities that could suffer include entrepreneurial activities, export-led growth, innovation etc.

He goes on to argue that where there is a wage premium in a natural resource-driven industry like the Oil and Gas industry, it creates a significant incentive for entrepreneurs and rent-seekers to invest in trying to gain access to the economic rents that flow from the industry (unlike the simple Dutch Disease phenomenon where wages rise across all sectors of an economy for workers with comparable skillsets) which lead to a decline in growth and increases in prices in the wider economy.

The availability of resource rents often leads to corruption which in turn slows economic growth even further as investible surpluses are misappropriated.

Dietz, Neumayer and De Soysa (2007) argues that it is ultimately policy failure that underpins the natural resource curse and I agree with them that resource rich countries can improve their weak sustainability and growth performance by fighting corruption and improving institutional quality by implimenting the United Nations Convention against corruption and by setting up Sovereign wealth funds to protect economic surpluses, aid diversification of the economy, generate yields from financial assets and generate wealth for future generations.

For the sake of completeness, I must draw attention to a very recent and significant meta-analysis on natural resources and economic growth by Havranek, Horvath and Zeynalov (2016), carried out to examine the so-called resource curse. They concluded that overall support for the resource curse hypothesis is weak when potential publication bias and method variability are considered and there is no consensus answer to demonstrate clear causation between natural resource abundance and its direct effects on long-term economic growth.

What Makes Rent-Seeking a Problem for Development?

Rent-seeking could be deemed to be unproductive or to lead to unproductive activities by definition and reduces the otherwise investible economic rents which in turn reduces the potential for economic growth and development over time. Other problems include the following:

1. It could incentivise corruption of public officials who may be motivated to share in the rent-seeking gains and undermine the provision of collective/common good.

2. Lobbying of policy decision-makers may protect interests (rents) of one lobbying group over another group leading to GNP reduction at the expense of innovation and lower prices.

3. Rent-seeking may worsen wealth inequality in society because wealth is redistributed rather than created and widens the gap between the rich and the poor which could lead to social/civil unrest/political instability.

4. It could be perceived as an indication of an economy in decline with higher risks for investors leading to continual decline in government taxation revenues with direct adverse consequences for infrastructure

spending, research & development funding and the provision of public services.

5.   Rent-seeking activities discourage market competition and may disincentivise the much needed foreign investment that is essential for accelerating export-led economic growth, technological progress, innovation transfer and production cost reduction.

The graph below by Murphy, Shleifer and Vishny (1991) depicts the potential reduction in economic growth (GDP per capita) due to rent-seeking activities in the USA over a 30 year period.

The Cost of Rent-Seeking: Actual and Potential Economic Growth

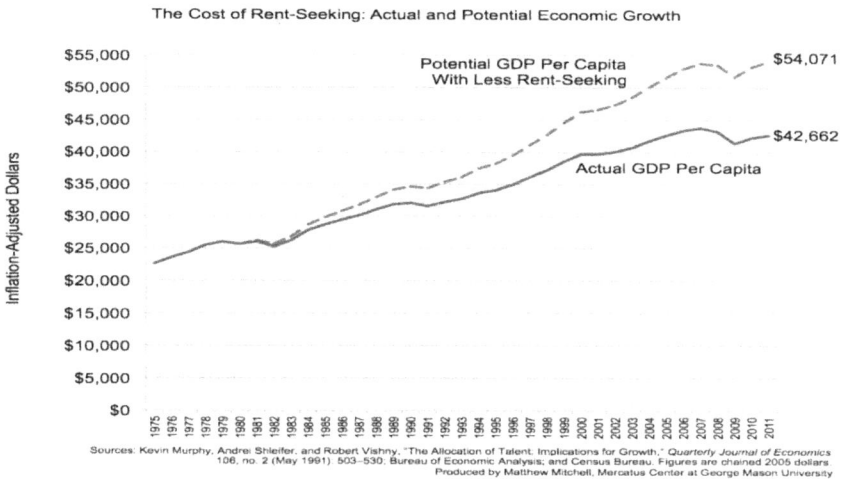

Sources: Kevin Murphy, Andrei Shleifer, and Robert Vishny, "The Allocation of Talent: Implications for Growth," *Quarterly Journal of Economics* 106, no. 2 (May 1991): 503–530; Bureau of Economic Analysis; and Census Bureau. Figures are chained 2005 dollars. Produced by Matthew Mitchell, Mercatus Center at George Mason University

What Makes Rent-Seeking Helpful?

1. Through the privatisation of state owned assets in sectors such as Housing, Healthcare, Power, Transport, Agriculture etc, private sector investors (rent-seeking and profit-seeking) may be attracted to create sustainable markets and improve efficiency for the benefit of consumers and taxpayers.

2. Privileged government subsidies (budgetary allocation) can be targeted in the short run to develop new segments of the economy and diversify contributions to the GDP and build workforce capabilities, speeding up the development process of the economy which is beneficial in spite of the transfer contest costs (opposition rents), and wealth will be better distributed in the economy.

3. Emergency bailout loans for key industries (Banking, Automotive, Steel etc) can be justified in exceptional economic downturns to protect the wider economy from worse shocks, even though shareholders of the bailed-out firms would benefit much more than anyone else.

The Ways to Choose the Helpful Aspects

There are several policy frameworks that could be cited to aid development by boosting economic growth and reduce rent-seeking activities. The role of government in this context, according to the World Development Report (1987) is to provide modern infrastructure, to provide a stable incentive system and to ensure that government bureaucracy helps rather than hinders export growth.

Other helpful policies are outlined as follows:

1. The state must ensure export rules are liberal coupled with a stable incentive system (including land rights), as already mentioned, to drive economic growth as observed in the cases of the USA in the nineteenth century and South Korea and Taiwan in the 1970s and 1980s. In time, as the growth takes off, the rates of protection may be reduced. Exports also contribute to resource allocation according to comparative advantage. The most promising path to economic growth according to the World Development Report (1987) begins with a phase of import substitution followed by exportation of non-durable consumer goods and the inputs incentivise further exports creating more economic growth.

111

2. Reform trade policy - Adopt outward oriented trade strategies by lowering trade barriers, replacing quantitative restrictions with tariffs because it allows firms to operate in a less restrictive business environment allowing them to procure imported inputs more easily and it removes the incentive for unproductive activities. Maintaining credible currency exchange rates also enhances trade planning and viability.

3. Greater reliance on domestic private enterprise and less policy imposed distortion in labour and capital markets unless the policies are geared towards improving the quality of human capital and allocation of human capital for growth, as evidenced by Murphy, Shleifer and Vishny (1991) i.e. by incentivising the training of graduates and postgraduates in Science, Technology Engineering and Mathematics (STEM subjects) rather than Law, Journalism and Religion which lead to professions which are arguably less socially useful for economic growth or development.

4. Improve budgetary resource allocation to compel domestic businesses to become more efficient by competing with foreign firms and to open the economy to new opportunities while strengthening Anti-Corruption legislation and enforcement agencies in order to improve institutional quality, societal embeddedness and autonomy of a developmental state.

5. Change the rules of the game by making changes to taxation policies on assets i.e. having higher rates of capital gains tax for assets held for shorter periods and reduced rates for longer periods. Plugging tax-loopholes and cracking down on tax evasion at the same time could increase development possibilities and opportunities.

6. Legislate against monopolies, introduce Competition/Antitrust Laws, institute fair trade commissions and strengthen Competition

Commissions to objectively and independently regulate markets so they can award significant fines against profiteering corporations and guard against monopolies in the interest of consumers and taxpayers.

7. Privatise some state assets (Type 3 Rent-seeking opportunity), maintain strategic state-ownership of key infrastructure/assets and develop cross-party consensus around long-term industrial strategies to minimise the effects of short term political investment decisions, unproductive bidding contests and reduce market uncertainty.

8. Establish a central bank funded Sovereign wealth funds to protect economic surpluses, aid diversification of the economy, generate yields from financial assets and generate wealth for future generations from the initial invested dividends/resource rents in a natural resource abundant economy and help to avoid the so-called resource curse of slow export driven growth, high commodity prices and slow development.

9. Mandate sworn asset declaration and tax return disclosure for all elected politicians, politicians seeking public office and senior civil servants periodically and institute an independent quasi-non-governmental organisation to monitor and scrutinise political party funding to discourage cronyism, unproductive rent-seeking contests and a culture of patronage.

Conclusions

Rent-seeking has been defined comprehensively and has been shown to have quantifiable economic impacts most of which are obstacles to economic development. However, it has also been shown to be a rational entrepreneurial response which can be channelled by strategic state intervention in developmental states to productive activities that stimulate economic growth.

Several government policy frameworks have been outlined to show how export driven economic growth and development may be achieved and sustained and how rent-seeking activities may be discouraged for the common good.

Appendix 1: Wealth of Selected Nations by GDP 2015

COUNTRY	GDP (USD B$)	RANKING
USA	17,846	1
China	10,866	2
UK	2,848	5
India	2,073	7
Brazil	1,774	9
Russia	1,326	13
Saudi Arabia	646	20
Nigeria	481	23
South Africa	312	32
Portugal	198	44

Data Source: World Bank Group 11/10/2016

Appendix 2: Wealth of Top 10 Corporations by 2015 Turnover

CORPORATION	REVENUE (USD B$)	RANKING
Walmart	482	1
China Grid	330	2
CNPC -China	299	3
Sinopec Grp	294	4
Royal Dutch Shell	272	5
Exxon Mobil	246	6
Volkswagen	237	7 (10.1MC)
Toyota	237	8 (10.3MC)
Apple	234	9
BP	226	10

Data Source: Fortune 500 20/07/2016

Notes:

1. Walmart's Turnover is greater than the GDP of Nigeria (the 23rd largest economy).

2. 3 out of the 4 largest corporations are owned by the Chinese state with a cumulative turnover of almost $1 Trillion ($923 Billions).

3. The 10th largest corporation BP has a turnover greater than the GDP of Portugal.

References

Belassa, B. (1988). The Lessons of East Asian Development: An Overview. *Economic Development and Cultural Change.* 36 (3), p277 - 289.

Baumol, W.J. (1990). Entrepreneurship: Productive, Unproductive, and Destructive. *Journal of Political Economy.* 98(5) (1), p893 - 921.

Bhagwati, J. (1982). Directly Unproductive, Profit-Seeking (dup) Activities. *Journal of Political Economy,* 90(5), P988 – 1002.

Buchanan, J.M. and Tullock, G. (1962). *The Calculus of Consent: Logical Foundations of Constitutional Democracy.* Michigan: University of Michigan Press. p22.

Congleton, R.D., Hillman, A.L. and Konrad, K.A. (2008). *40 years of Research on Rent Seeking 2 Applications: Rent Seeking in Practice.* Berlin: Springer. p23 - 39.

David, P.A. and Wright,G. (1997). Increasing Returns and the Genesis of American Resource Abundance. *Industrial and corporate change.* 6 (1), p203 - 245.

Dietz, S., Neumayer, E. and De Soysa, I. (2007). Corruption, the resource curse and genuine saving. *Environment and Development Economics.* 12 (1), p33 - 53.

Evans, P. (1995). *Embedded Autonomy: States and Industrial Transformation.* Princeton: Princeton University Press. p43 - 60 & 228.

Havranek, T., Horvath, R. and Zeynalov, A. (2016). Natural Resources and Economic Growth: A Meta-Analysis. *World Development*. 88 (1), p134 - 151.

Krueger, A.O. (1974). The Political Economy of the Rent-Seeking Society. *The American Economic Review*. 64 (3), p291 - 303.

Mayshar, J., Moav, O., Neeman, Z. and Pascali, L. (2015). Cereals, Appropriability and Hierarchy. *Centre for Economic Policy Research*. DP10742 (1), p47 - 49.

Moore, M. (2004). Revenues, State Formation and the Quality of Governance in Developing Countries. *International Political Science Review*. 25 (3), p297 - 319.

Murphy, K.M., Shleifer, A. and Vishny, R.W. (1991). The Allocation of Talent: Implications for Growth. *The Quarterly Journal of Economics*. 106 (2), p503 - 530.

Sachs, J.D. and Warner, A.M. (2001). The curse of natural resources. *European Economic review*. 45 (4-6), p827 - 838.

The World Bank (1987). *World Development Report*. London: Oxford University Press. p76 & 169.

Tullock, G. (1967). The Welfare Costs of Tariff, Monopolies and Theft. *Western Economic Journal*. 5 (3), p224 - 232.

Tullock, G. (1980). Efficient rent seeking. In: Buchanan, J.M et al *Toward a theory of rent-seeking society*. College Station: Texas A&M University Press. p97 - 112.

Smith, A. (1776). Of the Principle that gives occasion to the division of labour. In: *An Inquiry into the Nature and Causes of the Wealth of Nations*. London: Strahan & Cadell. p1.

PAPER 3

Essay Topic (Option 2): 'HRM policies and practices aim to contribute to the competitive success of the firm by developing, nurturing and rewarding the firm's most valuable asset, its employees. Yet the spread of Zero-hours contracts, bogus self-employment and low wages suggests that HRM managers have little influence over the popular cost-minimization business model preferred by many firms'.

A discussion by Adrian Ikeji

Date: 12/12/2016

Essay Word Count: 3250

Introduction

Since the early decades of the 20th Century and the formalisation of lessons learned from workplace management experiments, such as the Hawthorne effect and the Wiring room experiment, which demonstrated that observation of workers may improve performance and workers are not solely motivated by economic considerations, respectively, Human Relations Theory has evolved considerably. Human Resources Management (HRM) functions have developed to cover all aspects of the employee life cycle – from recruitment to termination/retirement through all the developmental and transactional phases in between, and has become a core strategic function of business managers everywhere, in the pursuit of a competitive advantage, profitability and sustainability.

The statement which is the topic for discussion identifies three current trends namely: a) The spread of Zero-hours contracts. b) The spread of "bogus" self-employment. c) The spread of low wages. The statement presupposes a link between HRM practices and the choice of a low-cost business strategy by firms and suggests that HR managers have little influence over the strategic choice because of the aforementioned trends.

This essay aims to clarify the aims of HRM, investigate the presupposed link between HRM practices and business strategic performance, explore the trends identified in the statement and lastly the nature of the influence that HR managers have in light of the trends in the United Kingdom (UK) labour market. No distinction will be drawn between Human Relations Management and Human Resources Management because of the length constraint of this essay.

According to Clegg, Kornberger and Pitsis (2016 p.195), *"HR and HRM do not occur in a vacuum; the HR manager cannot simply assume that anything goes, because HR occurs in specific contexts undergoing constant change: government policy, industrial relations, unionization, social attitudes, globalization, demographic changes, immigration, technological changes and so on, all affect the ability to perform and implement the major HR functions"*.

Their statement is pertinent and very true today as modern employment trends and cultural changes in the economy become more complex (for recent political reasons) and as the pace of change gets even faster with advances in technologies. The impacts have to be considered carefully for clarity and so that adequate preparation can be made to challenge concerning aspects or to protect businesses from avoidable costs and workers from exploitation. Modernity sometimes leaves an inevitable void or gap in meaning and creates insecurity about identity which employment or work may fill, but as Grey (2013 p.58) points out, managers have the capacity to represent and intervene in particular ways. Some of which will be made clear by the end of this essay.

Perception of HRM

HRM may be perceived as pervasive because as Grey (2013) suggests, HRM seeks to control through human relationships (rather than avoiding them) which may not always be agreeable with every employee or worker. Conversely, it can be perceived as a way of acknowledging and controlling the irrepressible informal side of the organisation in line with the formal parts and purposes of the organisation.

It proffers practicable management solutions to problems experienced with pure scientific management such as employee relations disputes, absenteeism, poor work quality, sabotage, high staff turnover etc. and it provides an essential framework for ensuring the legal compliance of all employment practices.

I agree that HRM is imperative today and provides the acceptable toolkit for effective organisational management in a constantly changing social, economic, political and environmental landscape. HR managers have to ensure that their actions and the actions of agents of firms (decision-makers and others) are ethical and lawful and that all management practices and policies are presented and perceived to be helpful rather than harmful to the firm and its most valuable asset, its people.

Strategic HRM and Business Performance

Martel, Gupta, Caroll and Stephen (1996) studied the effectiveness of HRM within the strategic framework of different businesses in the United States of America and they tested the linkage with performance, defined by contribution to the companies' bottom line –strategic objective. The study was done using moderated regression analysis on questionnaire responses from a sample of 115 (General Manager Level) strategic business units of Fortune 500 companies with a mixture of cost leadership (cost-minimization) and differentiation (market distinction) business models.

16 HRM practices pertaining to four HR policy areas (staffing, performance appraisal, compensation and training) were tested and their analysis yielded the following conclusions:

1. Eight strict universal relationships were found which were spread across performance appraisal and staffing policy areas with insignificant correlations in other areas, although training was found to have a positive link at the low-cost end of the business strategy spectrum.

2. Only two HRM practices demonstrated a positive relationship contingent upon the business strategy setting. They are: a)

Performance in Differentiation firms is more highly related to the use of objective performance criteria when evaluating executives than in cost minimization firms. b) The high utilization of performance appraisal results is positively related to performance but the relationship is more positive among Differentiation firms.

The results of the study demonstrate that the main proposition of strategic HRM theory linking HRM practices and policies to business performance is valid, regardless of the business model adopted by the firm.

The Rise of Zero-Hours Contracts

According to the guidance from the UK Government Department for Business, Energy and Industrial Strategy (2015), the term Zero-hours contract is a non-legal term used to describe many different types of casual agreements between an employer and an individual. Individuals on these contracts (also known as atypical, contingent, casual etc) are entitled to all statutory rights that apply to workers (not employees) without exception, and are entitled to wages at least equal to the national minimum wage/ national living wage, paid annual leave, rest breaks and protection from discrimination. Exclusivity clauses preventing a worker from taking other employment or doing work for other employers are prohibited under the Small Business Enterprise Act 2015.

Some 'appropriate use' examples are given in the guidance to include: new businesses, seasonal work, unexpected sickness, special events and service testing. 'Improper use' examples include: permanent arrangements, regular hours of work over a continuous period of time e.g. 12 months, employers trying to avoid obligations/responsibilities and for core business operations.

In a joint report from HRZone, ACAS and CIPD (2015) on workplace trends, the following points (covering usage, rationales, benefits and disbenefits and trends) were gleaned from articles written by contributors representing the Advisory, Conciliation and Arbitration Service (ACAS), the Chartered Institute of Personnel and Development (CIPD) and the Trade Union Congress, regarding the use of atypical contracts:

1. The 2014 ACAS Workplace Employment Relations Study shows that there was an increase from 4% (in 2004) to 8% (in 2011) of organisations using Zero-hours contracts. In the same study 97% of all employees and workers are protected or covered by statutory provisions, ACAS codes of practice or workplace policies.

2. The 2014 CIPD survey shows that 36% (40% of large companies) of all UK organisations use casual workers. Since the 2008 economic downturn most organisations cite cost efficiency and uncertain business conditions as reasons for using atypical contracts and more than half of all organisations offering them indicate to the CIPD that their main reason for using them is – improved ability to manage fluctuations in demand.

3. A third of organisations see it as an opportunity to offer flexible working arrangements. A quarter of employers see it as opportunity to improve productivity through more effective deployment. 30% of employers claim they use it to fill skills gaps in the core workforce. Some other reasons cited from the Agile Future Forum case studies, referred to by CIPD, are that atypical workforces offer the benefit of greater organisational agility (ability to respond to change), and increased quality of outputs through diversity of skills and ability to attract talent.

4. A 2013 CIPD survey showed that 47% of workers are satisfied with having no minimum contracted hours and 27% of workers are dissatisfied with Zero-hours contracts.

5. 35% of organisations indicate to the CIPD that inconsistencies in the quality of work is a business concern of atypical contracts but only a third of organisations conduct performance appraisals. Only 54% of workers on Zero-hours contracts have a line manager compared to the UK overall workforce average of 80%.

6. The 2014 ONS Labour survey shows that since 2008 there have been 300000 more temporary and casual workers. 1.4 million Zero-hours contracts in 2014 with increasing use by Airline Pilots, Lecturers, School Teachers, Social Care workers and low-skilled jobs.

7. Workers' rights are becoming harder to enforce, according to the TUC, because of the increasing power imbalance in the workplace attributed to atypical contracts and the introduction of Employment Tribunal (ET) fees, introduced in July 2013. There has been a 79% drop in ET applications/claims since the fees were introduced.

8. The TUC contributor also suggests that atypical workers are most likely to be earning low wages, not paying much in taxes and National Insurance (NI) contributions and not spending much either.

9. It is noted that atypical workers often do not have any sickness entitlements, company maternity pay or company retirement plans and as a result would only have recourse to state benefits.

10. Lastly, there was reference to research carried out by Cambridge University in 2014 (Burchell and Wood, 2014) which shows that a range of flexible employment practices used in US and UK Supermarkets (including Zero-hours contracts) cause widespread

anxiety disorders, stress and depression in workers as a result of persistent financial and social uncertainty.

In light of the increasing popularity of the Zero-hours contracts (and other atypical arrangements) with employers, for understandable reasons, and the disparate implications for workers, ranging from flexible working arrangements, convenience and variety, at the positive end to insufficient income, persistent uncertainty, poor future planning support and health problems at the negative end of the spectrum, it is clear to me that HRM interventions will be required going forward to help maintain the ethics and sustainability of organisational strategies.

Principally, the HRM professionals are best placed to ensure that there is fairness, consistency and compliance in decision-making processes in the changing workplace. HR practices and policies may have to be updated sooner rather than later, in my view, to address the organisational commitment and cultural problems, such as declining worker loyalty, weak ties, lower emotional identity, low likelihood of continuance and the potential for opportunistic sabotage, which may only worsen as the popularity of these atypical contracts grow for short-term economic reasons.

.

Developments in the Gig Economy

There are three recognised statuses of employment in UK employment law and they can be characterised thus: a) The employee – employed by an employer, benefits from full contractual and statutory benefits and enjoys the full range of employment rights. b) The worker – contracted by an employer (typically for a fixed period or atypically as alluded to previously) and has basic statutory rights and fewer protections. c) The self-employed individual – earns income transactionally or under contract but is liable to pay taxes directly to the state and is only protected from discrimination in the context of employment. The so-called gig-economy is made up of temporary job positions available to self-employed individuals for short-term engagements.

Work in the gig economy is often provided by a new type of business enterprise known as non-employing firms i.e. businesses that do not employ anyone and are managed by information technology proprietors using digital platforms (mobile phone apps and the internet typically) to connect with customers and providing goods and services at very competitive rates via a self-employed workforce on zero hours contracts. The trouble is the term self-employed workforce is an oxymoron and seems contradictory to the government's guidance on the appropriate use of such contracts.

Devlin (2016) analyses data from the Office of National Statistics (ONS) on non-employing firms and Transport for London (TfL) Taxi License data and reveals that:

a) The number of non-employing firms in the UK has increased by 28% since 2010.
b) The number of non-employing firms in London has increased by 72% since 2010.
c) The number of private hire licensed taxis (many part of the UBER workforce) in London has risen from 60,000 in 2010 to over 100,000 in 2016.

O'Connor (2015) highlights concerns and trends regarding bogus self-employment after a survey report from the Citizens Advice Bureau (CAB) – a state funded charity with 319 civil advice centres - warns that bogus self-employment is a hidden and growing problem in Britain caused by unscrupulous employers that are depriving the government from taxes and denying workers their rights by deliberately mislabelling workers as self-employed contractors, as evidenced by 10% of the 500 surveyed clients . The CAB chief executive is quoted as saying that workers are missing out on over £1000 per year because they legally should be official employees.

Trends identified by O'Connor include: a) Increasing legal and political disputes over employment status in the UK, US and Europe since the advent of mobile telephone business apps such as Uber, Deliveroo, Taskrabbit, JustEat, etc. b) Imminent government plans to review modern working practices (including self-employment) and strengthen rules. c) HMRC plans to crackdown on bogus self-employment as they estimate that £430 million in 2015 tax receipts could be lost due to non-compliance with rules against bogus self-employment (IR35).

On the 28th of October 2016, the judgment in case number: 2202551/2015 (Y. Aslam, J. Farrar and others against Uber B.V, Uber London Ltd and

Uber Britannia Ltd) was made public at the Central London Employment Tribunal. The tribunal found that the claimants had in fact been employed by Uber London Ltd as workers within the meaning of the Employment Rights Act 1996 and other statutory legislation. It also ruled that the claimants' working time was to be calculated and their unmeasured work be reckoned in accordance with the Working Time Regulations 1998 and the National Minimum Wage legislation, respectively. A remedy hearing is expected to be set for schedules of loss to be considered and for damages to be awarded. Uber went on record the next day to declare their intention of appealing the judgment.

If this landmark tribunal decision is not overturned on appeal, by a superior tribunal or court then it will have very significant implications for the 40,000 other Uber drivers on the same atypical contract and the estimated 460,000 other falsely classified self-employed individuals (Osbourne 2016) in the gig economy, as they will all be entitled to the National Living Wage and Holiday Pay, at least. The government would also be expecting to receive NI contributions from Uber and all the other firms, arguably mislabelled as non-employing firms, in the gig economy.

Booth (2016) records the widely expected and welcomed government announcement launching the HMRC specialist unit to investigate companies that opt out of giving workers employment protections by labelling them as agency staff or self-employed. In the report, the financial secretary to the Treasury reiterates the government's commitment to taking strong action where companies, to reduce their costs, force their staff down routes which deny them employment rights and benefits they are entitled to.

It is quite clear to see from the developments in the gig economy, chronicled above, that the political will and economic incentive for the government are in place to regulate activities in the gig economy. A by-product of the regulation may be better protection for the bogus self-employed workforce in the UK.

HR managers have a clear role to play in ensuring that businesses do not fall foul of any of the imminent statutory, contractual or taxation changes and to assist firms embracing new cost-effective business paradigms to mitigate their exposure to compensation and litigation costs by acting swiftly to review practices, policies and contracts in use at present.

Low Wages and Self-Employment

As has been seen in the two previous sections, there is increasing use of atypical contracts and the number of self-employed individuals is increasing for economic reasons. Low wages is a direct consequence of these trends because of a reduction of available working hours coupled with the expanding unskilled labour supply due to increasing immigration which is outpacing demand, slow economic growth and the slump in the value of the pound (which is leading to rising inflation).

Corlett (2016) has identified that typical earnings for the self-employed workforce were lower in 2014 -15 than in 1994 - 95 (20 years earlier) a fall of 15% compared to a rise of 14% in typical employee earnings.

From 2006 - 07 to 2013 -14, typical self-employment earnings fell by 32% (£100 per week). Corlett's findings were made by using the annual Family Resources Survey controlled by the Department for Works and Pensions.

The low wages trend means that HRM professionals need to use non-monetary rewards and recognition schemes and employee engagement activities, more effectively, to motivate workers to perform and feel valued. Ways to reduce occupational insecurity have to be devised also to mitigate the undesirable welfare consequences of the popular cost-minimization business model.

Conclusions

HR managers may have to be more proactive at recognising and addressing the needs (training, performance appraisal, voice, health, end of career etc) of atypical workers to change the perception of exploitation that is gaining traction in an increasingly cynical society because the statutory protections and guidelines are not sufficient at the moment to assure one, that some unethical exploitation of workers and rent-seeking (direct unproductive profiteering) is not going on.

HR managers have a clear role to play in ensuring that businesses do not fall foul of any of the imminent statutory, contractual or taxation changes and to assist firms embracing new cost-effective business paradigms to mitigate their exposure to compensation and litigation costs by acting swiftly to review practices, policies and contracts in current use.

Contrary to the suggestion made in the topic being discussed, I am confident that HRM professionals are and will continue to be instrumental and influential in promoting trust in the workplace and maintaining organisational culture, inclusive of the increasing number of atypical workers beyond the regulatory provisions for the long-term benefit of firms. They should have the dynamic capabilities to adjust to the current changes and have the strategic ability to create win–win solutions and support firms to develop workplce practices that allow for fairly balanced employment relationships, regardless of the business model adopted.

UK employment statutory provisions and codes of practice are in need of updating, partly because of the imminent brexit plans (and the Great Repeal Bill which may end the authority of all EU Laws and the employment rights that flow therefrom) but more crucially, imminent new primary legislation for atypical working arrangements. HR policies and practices need to be formulated, sooner rather than later, to take into account the major changes taking place in the working environment such as the growth of the gig economy, the popularity of contigent/atypical work and zero-hours contracts with firms, the growing income inequality and lower wages.

The new policies and statutory updates are particularly necessary to reflect the values and realities faced by young workers, 35 years of age and younger – generation -Y workers (Clegg, Kornberger and Pitsis, 2016) and other vulnerable worker groups, to enable them to continue in gainful employment with dignity and respect, as long as they are able to, and protect them from exploitation and misinformation because of their openness to new technologies (including the internet and other sources of information with varying levels of veracity), competition for jobs and need for flexibility.

I have no doubt that the government will do what is necessary to protect tax revenues.

References

Booth, R. (2016). Ministers order HMRC crackdown on 'gig economy' firms. [ONLINE] Available at: https://www.theguardian.com/politics/2016/oct/20/hmrc-launch-crackdown-gig-economy-firms-agency-self-employed-staff. [Accessed 9 December 2016]

Burchell, B and Wood, A. (2014). *Beyond Zero-hours: reducing the misery of insecure hours.* [ONLINE] Available at: https://sm.britsafe.org/beyond-zero-hours-reducing-misery-insecure-hours. [Accessed 12 December 2016]

Corlett, A (2016). The RF Earnings Outlook. [ONLINE] Available at: http://www.resolutionfoundation.org/app/uploads/2016/08/RF-Earnings-Outlook-Briefing-Q2-2016.pdf. [Accessed: 9 December 2016]

Clegg, S.R., Kornberger, M. and Pitsis, T.S. (2016). *MANAGING & ORGANIZATIONS An introduction to Theory and Practice.* 4th ed. London: SAGE. p161-195.

Department for Business, Energy and Industrial Strategy. (2015). *Zero hours contracts: guidance for employers. [ONLINE]* Available at: https://www.gov.uk/government/publications/zero-hours-contracts-guidance-for-employers/zero-hours-contracts-guidance-for-employers. [Accessed 10 December 2016].

Devlin, S. (2016). *Massive surge in London's gig economy.* [ONLINE] Available at: http://neweconomics.org/massive-surge-londons-gig-economy/. [Accessed 10 December 2016]

Employment Tribunal Service. (2016). *Aslam et al v Uber.* [ONLINE] Available at: https://www.judiciary.gov.uk/judgments/mr-y-aslam-mr-j-farrar-and-others-v-uber/. [Accessed 11th December 2016].

Grey, C. (2013). Human Relations Theory and People Management. In: Smy, K *A very short, fairly interesting and reasonably cheap book about STUDYING ORGANIZATIONS*. 3rd ed. London: SAGE Publications Ltd. p41-60.

HRZone, ACAS and CIPD. 2015). Workplace Trends of 2015: What they mean for you. [ONLINE] Available at: http://www.acas.org.uk/media/pdf/t/e/Workplace-trends-of-20151.pdf. [Accessed 9 December 2016]

Martell, K., Gupta, A. and Carroll, S.J., (1996). Human resource management practices, business strategies, and firm performance: A test of strategy implementation theory. *Ibar,* 17(1), pp. 18.

O'Connor, S. (2015). 'Bogus' self-employment deprives workers of their rights. *FT.com. Available via ABI/INFORM GLOBAL database.* [Accessed 11 December 2016]

Osbourne, H. (2016). Uber loses right to classify UK drivers as self-employed. [ONLINE] Available at: https://www.theguardian.com/technology/2016/oct/28/uber-uk-tribunal-self-employed-status. [Accessed 9 December 2016]

PAPER 4

Report Title: The impact of trade on economic growth in Nigeria (an emerging economy)

Report by Adrian Ikeji

Date: 14/02/2017

Word Count: 2731

Introduction

This essay aims to explore the impact of trade on the economic growth of an emerging economy of my choice. In order to select a suitable country to analyse, I referred to the commonly cited definition. According to Hoskisson et al (2000 p. 249), "Emerging economies are low-income, rapid growth countries using economic liberalization as their primary engine for growth".

Since the turn of the millennium when Hoskisson's list of 64 emerging economies was compiled - based on the macro-economic indicators - the global economy has experienced a severe shock as a result of the 2008 banking crisis, which led to a slowdown in economic activities and reductions in commodity prices on a global scale.

The economic recovery has been on-going for almost a decade now and some of the political and economic consequences still remain to be seen. This situation has meant that some countries which were previously characterised by their rapid growth are now battling to stave off economic recessions or are struggling to emerge from recessions. However, country income classifications (by the World Bank) and the popularity of the economic liberalization strategy for growth have remained unchanged, so I have chosen a country with all the aforementioned considerations in mind as well as the country's potential for future rapid growth.

My case study will focus on Nigeria; an emerging economy classified by the World Bank as a lower middle income economy in the sub-Saharan region of Africa. It has been a member of the World Trade Organization (WTO) since the organisation's inception on the 1st of January 1995 and it has had a relatively stable democratic government since 1999. Nigeria is cited on the BBVA Bank's (2014) watch-list of 11 developing countries forecast to add more to global growth in the next decade than Italy (the smallest G7 nation).

The theoretical relationship between trade and economic growth has been established for over two centuries. The trade theories posited by Adam Smith (Absolute Advantage of a country's production efficiency for a given product), David Ricardo (Comparative Advantage of specialized efficient production combined with the importation of goods from other countries with other specializations) and Eli Heckscher and Bertil Ohlin (Factor Endowment leading to comparative advantage of production) tell us simply, according to Hill (p161, 2014) that, "…a country's economy may gain if its citizens buy certain products from other nations that could be produced at home. The gains arise because international trade allows a country to specialize in the manufacture and export of products that can be produced most efficiently in that country, while importing products that can be produced more efficiently in other countries".

More recently, Kim and Lin (2009) retested the empirical link between trade and growth using a threshold regression method with instrumental variables such as national income levels, trade openness, productivity and investment. They found that trade impacts growth partly through its effects on capital accumulation, productivity and investment. In general terms, trade liberalisation effectively forces the government to reform programmes under the pressure of international competition. However, opening up to trade might actually reduce long-run economic growth if an economy specialises in sectors with dynamic comparative disadvantage regarding potential productivity growth or in sectors where technological innovators are largely exhausted.

Trade was shown to have a negative effect on the aforementioned independent variables in low-income countries because low-income countries tend to have worse environments for trade, such as inadequate legal systems, inadequate protection of property rights and more distorted government policies, which do not encourage investment and technological innovations, relative to higher- income countries.

Their work suggests that lower-income countries like Nigeria may have difficulties reaping the benefits of trade on growth through greater investment and higher productivity growth alone. They conclude that the relationship between trade and growth may be driven by deeper determinants of growth rather than trade itself and causality remains unproven.

I expect my case study to provide further support to their conclusions and shed some light on some complementary determinants that impact the economic growth model.

Trade and Growth Description of Nigeria

Nigeria has the largest population in Africa and its economy is also the largest in Africa. According to the International Monetary Fund (IMF) (2016), the economic activity in the country was projected to contract by 2% in 2016, as the economy adjusted to foreign currency shortages as a result of lower crude oil receipts, weak investor confidence etc. Nigeria has been a member of the Organisation of Petroleum Exporting Countries (OPEC) since 1971 and currently has a maximum Crude Oil production capacity of 2.5 million barrels per day (more than Brazil).

In terms of Gross Domestic Product (GDP) converted to international dollars purchasing power parity (PPP), the Nigerian economy is estimated to be worth $1.093 Trillion by the World Bank (2017) making it the 20th largest economy by this measure (10 places ahead of South Africa – which curiously is a member of the G20 and a member of the BRICS group of leading emerging economies) while GDP per capita is $5910. GDP PPP is arguably the most commonly used indicator by economists for comparing living conditions or the use of resources between countries and it gives credence to the idea that the BRICS categorisations may be out-dated.

According to Nigerian Government records (2016), Nigeria derives 70% of its government revenues from the Oil and Gas sector and 95% of export earnings. The GDP as at 2016 equated to 50.2%, 28.7% and 21.1% for the Services, Agricultural and Industrial sectors, respectively and the top contributing sub-sectors to the Real GDP were Crop Production (21.8%), Domestic Trade (19.8), Oil and Gas (8.2%, down from over 40% in 2011), Real Estate (8.2%) and Telecommunications (7.5%).

Its main export partners in 2016 were India (25.4%), USA (17.9%), France (10.7%) and Spain (10.5%), while its main import partners were China (27.2%), Belgium (18.8%), The Netherlands (17.0%) and USA (9.4%).

The dataset below provides a comprehensive record of the available indicative economic data spanning a period of 25 years from The World Bank (2017) and reveals a rapid increase in GDP linked to market liberalisation and international trade since the era of stable democratic governance began in 1999.

Nigeria Descriptor 1990 2000 2015

Economy			
GDP (current US$) (billions)	**30.76**	**46.39**	**481.07**
GDP growth (annual %)	12.8	5.3	2.7
Inflation, GDP deflator (annual %)	9.3	35.2	2.9
Agriculture, value added (% of GDP)	32	26	21
Industry, value added (% of GDP)	45	52	20
Services, etc., value added (% of GDP)	23	22	59
Exports of goods and services (% of GDP)	35	52	11
Imports of goods and services (% of GDP)	18	20	11
Business and markets			
Time required to start a business (days)	..	37	31
Domestic credit provided by financial sector (% of GDP)	21.9	10.0	23.1

145

Tax revenue (% of GDP)	..	1.5	1.5
Military expenditure (% of GDP)	0.8	0.8	0.4
Mobile cellular subscriptions (per 100 people)	0.0	0.0	82.2
Internet users (per 100 people)	0.0	0.1	47.4
High-technology exports (% of manufactured exports)	..	1	2

Global links			
Merchandise trade (% of GDP)	62	64	20
Personal remittances, received (current US$) (millions)	10	1,392	21,060
Foreign direct investment, net inflows (BoP, current US$) (millions)	588	1,140	3,129
Net official development assistance received (current US$) (millions)	255.1	173.7	2,476.2

World view Population, total (millions)	95.62	122.88	182.20
Population growth (annual %)	2.6	2.5	2.6
People: Life expectancy at birth, total (years)	46	47	53
Fertility rate, total (births per woman)	6.5	6.1	5.7
Prevalence of HIV, total (% of population ages 15-49) Environment	1.4	3.9	3.1
Urban population growth (annual %)	5.4	4.1	4.4
Energy use (kg of oil equivalent per capita)	695	700	773
CO2 emissions (metric tons per capita)	0.40	0.64	0.55
Electric power consumption (kWh per capita)	87	74	142

Fertility in the ten largest countries

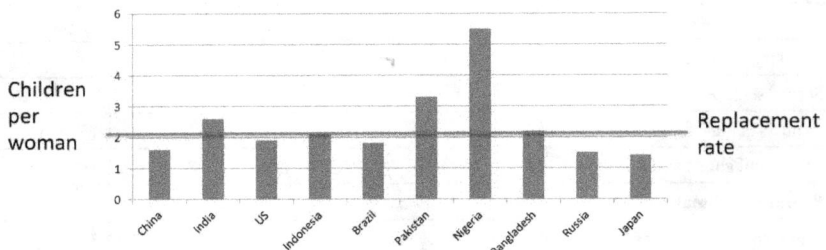

Children per woman — Replacement rate

China, India, US, Indonesia, Brazil, Pakistan, Nigeria, Bangladesh, Russia, Japan

Source: *UN World Population Prospects: The 2012 revision*

Sources of population growth to 2050

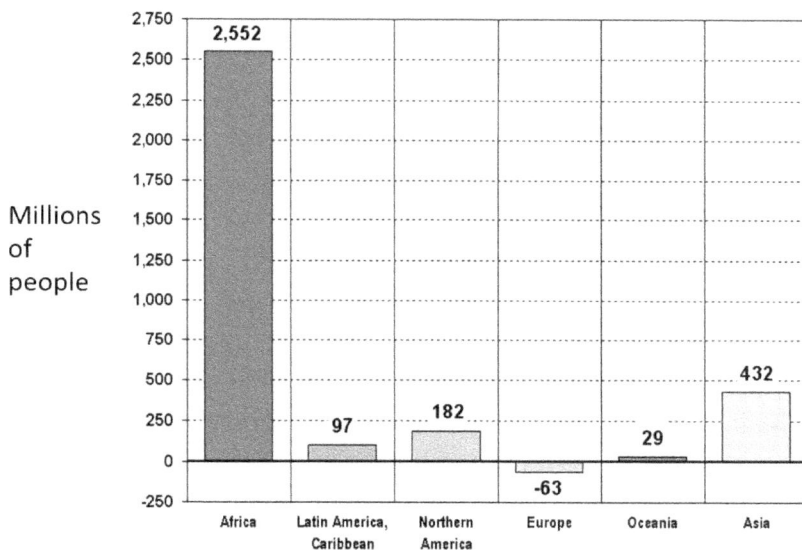

Source: United Nations, *World Population Prospects, The 2010 Revision*

Regional Trade Overview

The Economic Community of West African States (ECOWAS) came into being on 28 May 1975 following the ratification of the Treaty of Lagos bringing together 16 West African Countries to form a trade bloc. At the time, the trading bloc was created in response to challenges posed by the overdependence of member states on multinational corporations and advanced industrialised states (especially former colonial nations) and the regional problems of economic backwardness and a lack of development, as described by Okolo (1989).

Nigeria currently provides 55% of all exports from the region and 77% of exports to trading blocs and countries outside the African Continent. The European Union (EU) and the North Atlantic Free Trade Association (NAFTA) buy 60% of the exports, while 16% of exports go to Asian economies and 0.3% to Middle Eastern economies. The main exported products are fuels and by-products from extractive industries (75%), Cocoa products (5%), Precious minerals (3%), Rubber, Plastic products, Wood products, Edible fruits and fishery products (each accounting for 1%).

Regional imports consist mainly of refined petroleum products (24%), motor vehicles, agricultural and industrial machinery, mechanical and electrical appliances, steel products, pharmaceutical products etc. ECOWAS datasets (2012) show that Nigeria accounts for 41% of imports to the region, followed by Ghana (18%), Senegal (10%), Ivory Coast (10%). The 12 other countries account for 21%.

The chart below summarises the available cumulative regional exports data from 2001 to 2012 in US Dollars and depicts a rise, decline and stagnation indicative of serious endogenous and exogenous challenges and susceptibilities with direct consequences for regional economic growth.

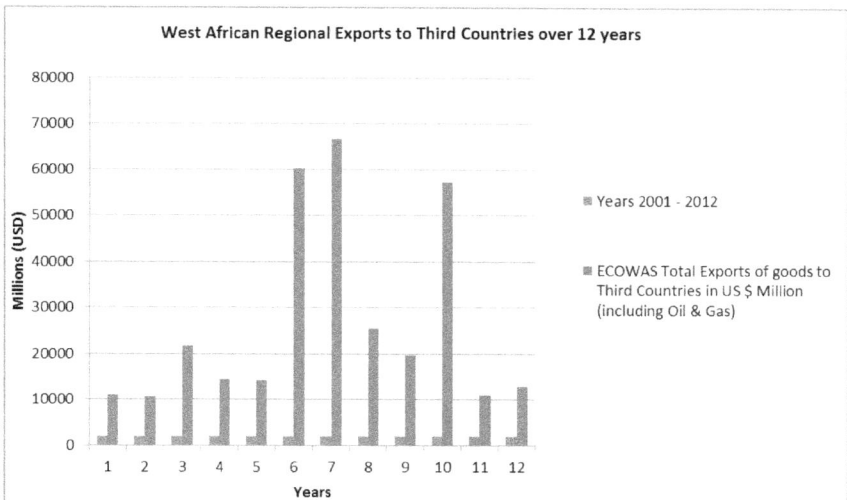

West African Regional Exports to Third Countries over 12 years

Legend:
- Years 2001 - 2012
- ECOWAS Total Exports of goods to Third Countries in US $ Million (including Oil & Gas)

Y-axis: Millions (USD)

X-axis: Years (1 through 12)

Regional Challenges and Susceptibilities

There is a significant lack of data on trade in services and as such, no meaningful analysis can be carried out on that aspect of economic activities beyond expecting that any such data would also show a decline not dissimilar to the chart on the previous page, following the 2008 global banking crisis and in line with the global falls in commodity prices and regional shocks from political instability. ECOWAS records (2017) state that trade in services within the region is hampered by institutional, regulatory and infrastructural constraints.

Okolo (1989) points out the main endogenous challenges that have restricted the trade potential and hampered export-driven economic growth in the region for over three decades now. They are: 1.Grossly inadequate transportation facilities in the region across all modes. 2. The diversity of currencies and the unreliability of exchange rates. 3. Multiple sub-regional trade liberalisation schemes with conflicting objectives. 4. Tariff preferences offered to European partners for primary products in exchange for duty free imports (because of historical/colonial ties) which undermines ECOWAS inter-regional trade integration and growth.

Local Empirical Study

Omoju and Adesanya (2012) applied a relevant econometric model to analyse a dataset from the Central Bank of Nigeria (CBN) covering GDP, Foreign Direct Investment (FDI), Terms of Trade, Government Expenditure and Currency Exchange Rate figures from the year 1980 to 2010.

The model was derived from the production function in which the level of a country's productivity is depicted by GDP and is explained by a linear relationship with the independent variables listed above. The test was carried out (with minor adjustments to the dataset) using the Linear Least Square Regression Method in a similar fashion to a previous study for 42 developing countries by Karbasi, Mohamadi and Ghofrani (2005), in order to ascertain the controlling parameters for testing the hypothesis based on established theory, in this emerging economy.

Predictably, the model demonstrated an 84% explanatory relationship (coefficient of determination of 0.84) and all the parameters were positively/directly related to GDP. A one unit rise in foreign trade was shown to increase GDP by 0.56 units while a unit increase in FDI, government spending and currency exchange rates increased GDP by 0.338, 0.323 and 0.004 units respectively.

The findings are used to justify policy recommendations put forward in the conclusion to encourage the Nigerian Government to harness the growth benefits of increasing returns to scale by creating a more conducive economic environment to attract more FDI, increase foreign trade, increase investment in infrastructure projects and stabilise exchange rates.

The causality question between trade and growth remains unanswered despite the strong relationship that exists but it has become clear that factors beyond econometric models account for a significant proportion (16%) of the explanation; in political governance models, especially in a case like Nigeria where the Oil and Gas sector has such a dominant role for trade, growth and development in the domestic and regional economy.

Overcoming the Natural Resource Curse

According to Sachs and Warner (2001), most current explanations for the curse have a crowding out rationality which is described as the activities linked to the abundance of natural resources stifling out other activities that could create growth and concluding that the abundance of natural resources could harm economic growth. The activities that could suffer include entrepreneurial activities, export-led growth, innovation etc.

He goes on to argue that where there is a wage premium in a natural resource-driven industry like the Oil and Gas industry, it creates a significant incentive for entrepreneurs and profit-seekers to invest in trying to gain access to the economic rents that flow from the industry (unlike the simple Dutch Disease phenomenon where wages rise across all sectors of an economy for workers with comparable skillsets) which lead to a decline in growth and increases in prices in the wider economy.

Nigeria falls squarely into the group of countries that have experienced the symptoms described above. The availability of resource rents often leads to corruption which in turn slows economic growth even further, as investible surpluses are often misappropriated. However, Nigeria (with its past record of squandered or misappropriated rents and untapped growth potential) can no longer afford to be ambivalent about the type of nation it has to be, to not only survive future shocks to the global economy but also to play its part in shaping geopolitics and the political economy of the next century, as its voice and economic significance increases.

Dietz, Neumayer and De Soysa (2007) argues that it is ultimately policy failure that underpins the natural resource curse and I agree with them that resource rich countries like Nigeria can improve their growth performance by continuing to fight corruption and improve institutional quality by fully implementing the United Nations Convention against corruption and strengthening anti-corruption agencies.

Furthermore, by increasing fiscal allocations to the Sovereign Wealth Fund (SWF) in line with oil price rises the government may better protect economic surpluses, aid diversification of the trade offering, generate yields from financial assets, generate wealth for future generations and grow the economy further.

Conclusions

I have shown that trade has a real and positive impact on economic growth in Nigeria and the impact is amplified by complementary political and demographical determinants.

The role of government in the context of economic growth, according to the World Development Report (1987) is to provide modern infrastructure, to provide a stable incentive system and to ensure that government bureaucracy helps rather than hinders export growth. However, this case study has shown that in a resource rich emerging economy, liberalized trade policies can be a more productive and efficient engine for economic growth when supported by improved institutional quality and governance structures. Also, targeted and sustained government spending on infrastructure provision, better regional co-operation, capitalising on favourable demographics and seeing through reforms to diversify revenue streams, modernise the tax base and increasing the absorptive capacity of the market will be beneficial.

Some other note-worthy policy frameworks are outlined below:

1. The state could ensure export and import rules are liberalized further and coupled with a stable and secure incentive system for entrepreneurs (including strengthened land and property rights) to drive economic growth in a similar way to the cases of the USA in

the nineteenth century and South Korea and Taiwan in the 1970s and 1980s respectively.

2. Ensure that the SWFs are replenished and built up as oil prices rise and the economy returns to growth. This would help to protect the fiscal surpluses and help to fund the extension of the diversification plan for the economy. It may also enable the acquisition of strategic assets regionally and in other emerging market economies to speed up the industrialisation process and improve technological spillovers.

Evidently, the Nigerian economy now looks well placed to emerge forcefully from its recession, in 2017 with greater resilience to forge even greater trading relationships across the globe as opportunities are presented by the dynamic political economy in the Triad countries (especially in the EU, UK and North America), other emerging economies and in Africa.

Appendix 1: Wealth of Selected Nations by Gdp 2015

Country	GDP (USD B$)	Ranking
USA	17,846	1
China	10,866	2
UK	2,848	5
India	2,073	7
Brazil	1,774	9
Russia	1,326	13
Saudi Arabia	646	20
Nigeria	481	23
South Africa	312	32
Portugal	198	44

Data Source: World Bank Group 11/02/2017

References

BBVA Bank. (2014). EAGLEs Economic Outlook. Available: https://www.bbvaresearch.com/KETD/fbin/mult/2014_EAGLEs_Economic_Outllok-Annual_tcm348-437158.pdf?ts=3132014. Last accessed 12th Feb 2017.

Dietz, S., Neumayer, E. and De Soysa, I. (2007). Corruption, the resource curse and genuine saving. Environment and Development Economics. 12 (1), p33 - 53.

ECOWAS. (2016). Regional Trade Statistics. Available: http://www.ecowas.int/doing-business-in-ecowas/import-and-export/. Last accessed 12th Feb 2017.

Hill, C.W. (2014). International Business: Competing in the Global Marketplace. 10th ed. Glasgow: McGraw-Hill Education. p159 - 179.

Hoskisson, R.E., Eden, L., Lau, C.M., Wright, M . (2000). Strategy in Emerging Economies. Academy of Management. 43 (3), p249 .

IMF. (2016). Uncertainty in the Aftermath of the UK Referendum. Available: https://www.imf.org/external/pubs/ft/weo/2016/update/02/#P39_12325. Last accessed 10th Feb 2017.

Karbasi, A., Mohamadi, E. and Ghofrani, S. (2005), Impact of foreign direct investment and trade on economic growth. In Economic Research Forum: 12th Annual Conference, 19th-21st December, Cairo, Egypt.

Kim, D & Lin S. (2009). Trade and Growth at Different Stages of Economic Development. Journal of Development Studies. 45 (8), p1218 - 1221.

Nigerian Government. (2016). Foreign Trade Statistics Q3 2016. Available: http://nigerianstat.gov.ng/report/472. Last accessed 14th Feb 2017.

Okolo, J. (1989). Obstacles to Increased Intra-ECOWAS Trade. International Journal. 44 (1), p171 - 214.

Omoju, O and Adesanya, O. (2012). Does trade promote growth in developing countries? Empirical Evidence from Nigeria. International Journal of Development and Sustainability. 1 (3), p1 - 11.

Sachs, J.D. and Warner, A.M. (2001). The curse of natural resources. European Economic review. 45 (4-6), p827 - 838.

The World Bank (1987). World Development Report. London: Oxford University Press. p76 & 169.

The World Bank Data Bank. (2017). Nigeria Country Profile. Available: http://databank.worldbank.org/data/views/reports/ReportWidgetCustom.aspx?Report_Name=CountryProfile&Id=b450fd57. Last accessed 11th Feb 2017.

UNIVERSITY OF LONDON

Birkbeck College

Adrian Okechukwu Ikeji

having completed the approved course of study and passed the
examinations has this day been admitted by Birkbeck College to the
University of London Degree of

MASTER OF SCIENCE

with Merit
in Management with International Business and Development

Master, Birkbeck College

Vice-Chancellor

1 February 2018